C0-AND-271

Out of the Basement

A Holistic Approach to Children's Ministry

Diane C. Olson

DISCIPLESHIP RESOURCES

P.O. BOX 340003 • NASHVILLE, TN 37203-0003
www.discipleshipresources.org

Cover design by Nanci Lamar.
Book design by Joey McNair.
Edited by Debra D. Smith and David Whitworth.
ISBN 0-88177-351-4
Library of Congress Catalog Card No. 00-108444

Scripture quotations, unless otherwise indicated, are from the New Revised Standard
Version of the Bible, copyright ©1989 by the Division of Christian Education of the
National Council of the Churches of Christ in the USA. All rights reserved. Used by
permission.

OUT OF THE BASEMENT: A Holistic Approach to Children's Ministry. Copyright ©
2001 Discipleship Resources. All rights reserved. No part of this book may be reproduced
in any form whatsoever, print or electronic, without written permission, except in the case
of brief quations embodied in critical articles or reviews. For information regarding
rights and permissions, contact Discipleship Resources Editorial Offices, P.O. Box 340003,
Nashville, TN 37203-0003, phone 615-340-7068, fax 615-340-1789, e-mail
mgregory@gbod.org.

DR351

Contents

Acknowledgments

I n July of 1999, several people in children's ministry from around the country were brought together to discuss their ministries with children. This book is a result of their hopes for a new, holistic resource. I am thankful for the input of each person at that initial meeting: Judy Eilders, Mary Alice Gran, Donna Gaither, Charlotte Matzinger, Judy Mayo, MaryJane Pierce Norton, Stephen Richards, and Clarice Setser. At the General Board of Discipleship, I thank Mary Alice Gran for her gentle persuasion to write this, Deb Smith for her patience with me and work as editor on this project, and Donna Gaither for her input into my descriptions of systems. Thanks to Linda Vogel, my friend and mentor who always believes in me, and to Phil Blackwell, for his story and encouragement for this book and life in general. I am thankful for all children, especially my own, David, Emily, and Amanda, who gave me lots of stories to write about as well as their support. Support of many kinds came from the colleagues in my clergy group and from the members and staff of First United Methodist Church at the Chicago Temple and all of the other churches where I have been a member or staff member over the years. I'm thankful for the heroes who have helped solidify my understandings of children's ministry, Laura Dean Friedrich, Joy Melton, D. J. Furnish, and Marian Wright Edelman. I am deeply grateful to the saints of First United Methodist Church of Windom, Minnesota, who, with my family, formed my faith and gave me the image of bringing children's ministries out of the basement. Without my sisters, Jan Reynolds and Linda Olson, I wouldn't have even begun to write this book. As my friends, confidantes, critics, and counselors, I am entirely grateful for all that they have done and continue to do in my life.

Introduction

People were bringing little children to him in order that he might touch them; and the disciples spoke sternly to them. But when Jesus saw this, he was indignant and said to them, "Let the little children come to me; do not stop them; for it is to such as these that the kingdom of God belongs."

Mark 10:13-14

I grew up in the church. My parents were very active laypeople, serving in a variety of leadership roles throughout my childhood. I spent many hours in our church, a lovely old building in Windom, Minnesota. The church sat not far from the park, where we played in vacation Bible school and skated in the wintertime. The church seemed huge to me, but when I've gone back to see those childhood places everything has been a lot smaller than I remember. For me, as a child, there were hundreds of steps leading up to the double doors of the sanctuary. As I remember, at ground level, to the left, there was a door leading to steps up to the "parlor," classrooms, choir room, and the pastor's study, and down to the basement. The basement had two large rooms with a sliding divider in the middle, used for all kinds of fellowship programs, potlucks, and classes. My Girl Scout troop met there for years. There was a kitchen and a hall that led past the nursery, toddler room, and bathroom to classrooms in the back. Many of the ministries of this church took place in the basement, especially those for children. It was somewhat humid year-round, and usually darker than the rest of the building, as basements are apt to be.

The people of this church (with Dad as chair of the building committee) built a lovely new building while I was away at college. Everything is on

Think back to the church of your childhood. What are your memories of church? How were children included and cared for?

one floor. When you enter that church, it feels like everything is accessible, but also like everything is equal in importance. Children's areas are front and center, easy to find and bright. Even the library is right where you can find it! I expect my mother had something to do with that, since she was the librarian at the time they built the new church.

I don't know that the people of this church consciously tried to bring their children's ministries out of the basement when they built their new church, but that is one of their accomplishments. The physical building indicates clearly that this is a place for children and adults. Now don't read this to say that basements are all bad, dark, or humid, and not good places for children. That's not my intent. In fact, there are ways to transform a basement so that it works well as a center space for children's ministries. I've seen some wonderful, well thought-out children's ministries happening in basements, as well as on every other floor you can think of. In my current church, First United Methodist Church of Chicago, most of the classroom ministry with children and small groups is done on the fourth floor of a twenty-five-story building! And our fellowship ministries, which account for most of the time our different generations spend interacting, are in the basement. But when I remember my "home" church in Windom, it seems to me that their experience is a good metaphor for the important need today in children's ministry. A metaphor, remember, is a verbal picture or image of a concept which helps one understand it, just as a symbol is a picture image. We need to bring ministry with, by, for, and to our children out of the basement and onto the first floor of our priorities, into the light, and into a place where it's equal to and accessible from our other ministries.

The title *Out of the Basement* also calls us to the careful consideration of the segmenting we so often do in our ministries. We put different ages in little cubbyholes, packaging our ministries to six-year-olds or sixty-year-olds as though the two should not be together. Think of your own church on any day of the week, but especially on Sundays. When are the generations together? How can they know each other, nurture and support each other if they spend most of their time apart from each other? I greatly respect the work of developmentalists and others who have taught us to separate and segregate our people so that individual needs can be clearly met in an efficient way. However, I think we have gone too far with that approach, taking the church into a place where we only know those people who are like us. It is time to teach and learn together, a family of faith united across the age span. Early in my ministry, I was frustrated by poor attendance in our summer age-grouped classes. Adults took a summer break from classes, and the children came once in a while. With the help of some interested laypeople, I developed a summer series around some of the heroes and heroines of the Bible, where each week we focused together as a church family on one person from the Bible. Usually, an

> **What can people of different generations teach each other? What values might a child teach an older person?**

adult told the story in some way, and we all worked together on some response to the story in drama, art, and music. Years later, I received a letter from one of the older men in that class, who wrote that the class had truly had an effect on his life. Leading the class helped him realize, he said, that he had gifts to offer children as well as adults. It made a difference in his life, and he thanked me for that experience. Our generations spend so much time apart from one another. The church must begin to think of new ways to bring them together.

Beginning at the General Conference of 1996, the bishops of The United Methodist Church focused on a challenging project. Called The Bishops' Initiative on Children and Poverty, this project is an effort to challenge the church to respond in new and holistic ways to the many issues of children and the poor. It is working to bring children's issues and ministries out of the metaphorical basement. The three primary goals of the initiative call us to reshape our church as an answer to the great needs of children and the poor, to develop and make available resources to help the church in these efforts, and to make known the grace and love of Jesus Christ through both what we say and what we do. To clarify and to launch the initiative, the bishops wrote a statement detailing its biblical and theological foundations. The document is radical, calling for an interpretation of the gospel in which the children are truly welcomed, affirmed, and loved as members of the community. The bishops expect it to cause us to reexamine all we do as a church, considering first how our behavior and our actions will affect the children and the poor. Out of that initiative have come a number of good, active changes, but mostly there has been a renewal of hope for the children of the church and world. This renewal of hope leads us to consider a holistic and comprehensive approach to ministry with all people. This renewal of hope is a first step out of the basement.

We are in a time in the history of the United States when there is a great urgency to lift our children's ministries out of the basement. Our children, those born in and between the years 1982 and 1999, are a huge demographic group. Called the "millennial generation" by planners and theorists, they are 76 million strong, more than any other generation. In 1998, there were more than 52 million students in elementary and high schools, a new record. By 2008, there will be more than 54 million (*Now Is the Time!* discussion guide, by Craig K. Miller and MaryJane Pierce Norton, Discipleship Resources, 1999, page 1). These children are people who have been born into the information age but seek to use resources and information to transform, not just inform. They are people who learn in many ways and at a fast pace, who are adept at choosing among many options and at multitasking. They value relationships, are multiethnic, and come out of changing family structures. Change is understood as a way of life and is an expectation. The church must place children's ministries on the first floor of our priorities so that we can begin to meet the needs of this generation before they find a substitute for the church in their lives.

Out of the Basement: A Holistic Approach to Children's Ministry is designed to help leaders in local congregations examine their systems of children's ministry in a comprehensive and holistic manner. It is not a cookbook with step-by-step instructions. Rather, this book considers the great value of relationships in children's lives and in their faith journeys. It presents a vision for children's ministry that recognizes children as growing disciples of Jesus Christ. I believe that all of the children of the church are disciples. There surely are none that Jesus would have excluded on the basis of age, gender, race, or ability to understand. All children are spiritual beings who seek meaning in their lives just as certainly as adults seek that meaning. It is through discipleship that meaning is found. Think of babies, who, without formal language, seek to understand the world around them, prodding and touching, tasting and examining with every sense. The adults and other children in their lives can surround them with love and the light of faith, shared in many ways. The love they return to those they have learned to trust is a part of their discipleship, a response to their inclusion in a family of faith. Yes, babies are too young to verbalize it, but they know God's love through the love of the community. If they are separated from it, they cannot learn it. We must bring our ministry with, by, and for children out of the basement, onto the main floor of the church's agenda in this new century. So let the children come, and do not stop them. For it is to such as these that the kingdom of God belongs.

Chapter 1
A Glimpse of the Kin(g)dom

"Truly I tell you, whoever does not receive the kingdom of God as a little child will never enter it." And he took them up in his arms, laid his hands on them, and blessed them.

Mark 10:15-16

As Christians, we have a great hope that we are bringing about the kingdom of God even as we journey toward it. The kingdom is here, among us, and it is also to come. As human beings, we have great difficulty understanding the concept of the kingdom of God. Jesus, in his parables about the kingdom, didn't give us a very clear explanation of it, and his disciples surely had trouble understanding it. Check, for instance, the parable of the seeds (Mark 4:1-20). There are comparisons to the kingdom, and suggestive verbal glimpses of what the kingdom might be like, but the picture remains somewhat vague. In Matthew 25:1-13, we read the parable of the ten bridesmaids. It begins by saying, "Then the kingdom of heaven will be like this." This brave statement is followed by a story with suggestion for us but not a clear and definitive description of the kingdom.

Further, in his teachings, Jesus taught us about a kind of kingdom that is different from our expectations of a kingdom, one where our relationships with each other and with God are more important than adherence to a rigid set of rules. For example, recall the stories of Jesus healing on the Sabbath. He taught us that the person in need of healing was more important than the prohibition against such action on the Sabbath. The rules of

What does the word *kingdom* mean to you? What does the word *kindom* mean?

belonging to the church did not come first; how we relate to others was (and is) primary.

Jesus turned things upside down. He showed us a way of existence where God is near and compassionate rather than being a fearsome judge who keeps a distance from us. God's reign is not like the rule of a king or queen or a socially elite ruling class, God's reign is a place of equality and care for each other. Jesus ate with sinners, touched the lepers, and ran the moneychangers from the Temple. He took on the role of a servant, washing his disciples' feet and instructing them to wash each other's feet. Jesus, as he had on many occasions, turned things upside down and used the language of "kingdom" to mean the absence of our views of societal hierarchy. In the kingdom of God, the world has a new order. The king is not a royal king but a servant king. People are not seen as better than each other for reasons of race, gender, or economic status. The poor are blessed, the hungry will eat, and those who weep will laugh (Luke 6:20-21). This way of being, where God reigns in an absence of "isms" (sexism, racism, and so forth), continues as a primary hope for Christians. We hope for God's kingdom to come on earth as in heaven, and we work toward that hope.

Working to bring about the kingdom, God's reign, is our hope for all of our ministries. However, for this culture in which we live and serve, the word *kingdom* still brings to mind earthly kings, monarchies, and domination. For this book, therefore, I have borrowed the word *kindom,* which came out of the movement for social justice in the church and world and is used by many people to provide an understandable alternative to the word *kingdom.* Kindom is like the image in the picture (called the Peaceable Kingdom) of the lion and lamb lying side by side, surrounded by other animals. The kindom is a way of being in which all are equal and loved, all are treated as sisters and brothers. The word *kin* implies relationship and family. People in the kindom are related to one another by their love for and by God. The kindom is what I imagine when I hear or sing "Jesus Loves the Little Children" or when I see the various versions of Jesus welcoming children in paintings and drawings. This is based on one of the fundamental Biblical references to children's ministries, Mark 10:13-16; Matthew 19:13-15; and Luke 18:15-17. "Let the little children come to me; do not stop them" (Mark 10:14). "And he took them up in his arms, laid his hands on them, and blessed them"(Mark 10:16). We are called to do the same in God's kindom.

One of my favorite books for children's and family ministry is *Regarding Children*. The authors cite Mark 10:16 as a call to churches to welcome children in order to bless them. They believe that the church needs to be a place "that practices to be a community where children are welcomed and honored as fully human and where there is compassion and justice for all persons" (from *Regarding Children.* © 1994 Herbert Anderson and Susan B. W. Johnson. Used by permission of Westminster John Knox Press).

Think of a time when, as a child, you were blessed by the words or actions of an adult in the church or at home.

How does the church bless children? What is the meaning of the word *bless*? Most of the time the word is used, it has a double meaning: to consecrate and to endow.

To consecrate is to make holy, to set apart by bestowing a religiously meaningful significance. Our children are consecrated when we honor them as fully human, not as immature adults or partial people. This requires us to learn from the children as well as to teach them. I remember a potluck Lenten dinner in my home church in Windom when I was about seven. I was there early with my parents, helping to set the tables. An older man in the church was putting the silverware at each place setting, and I corrected his placement of the knife and spoon, showing him the *right* way to set the table. Rather than be offended by my seven-year-old presumption of social graces, this loving man blessed me with praise, and praised my knowledge in front of other adults. I can still picture his smiling face in my mind, more than forty years later. I was, indeed, consecrated by his grace.

Children are consecrated when we praise them for their presence among us and accept their gifts and talents as an integral part of our life together. They are consecrated when we recognize that their vulnerability and needs are gifts among us and opportunities for the rest of the church community to serve. Every one of us has heard the cry of a child during a worship service. How often do we perceive that as a gift, a celebration of this life among us, rather than an interruption? The kindom of God includes crying infants as well as silent adults.

When we bless our children we also endow them with many gifts of the community. It is our responsibility as adult Christians to ensure the learning and faith development of children (and adults). To endow means to impart, to provide or bequeath, to pass along. We pass on the stories of the faith and of our community as a gift to them. My son loves to sing, and in high school he was one of the musicians at our annual ice cream social. He remembers with great appreciation the hours that Phil, one of the older men in our church, gave to teach him about the sound system and equipment so that his performance would be heard and understood as much as possible in an outdoor setting. They shared stories and technology throughout their

Was there a time when you were comforted by remembering a faith story or Bible verse learned in childhood?

short time together, and both were empowered by it. The knowledge was a blessing to my son, not only in content but also in the time shared with Phil.

Our hymn singing and rituals of worship give our children the gifts of constancy, familiarity, and safety. I can't number the times during crisis and pain in my life when I have relied on hymn texts and remembered tunes or on the Bible verses I memorized as a child. I remember being lost in a state park as a teenager, and hearing the words to the hymn "Jesus Loves Me" over and over in my mind until I was found.

Phil Blackwell, a pastor and dear friend, told me about one of his experiences of the comfort of remembered Bible verses. He is claustrophobic and was undergoing an MRI. The closeness of the walls of the huge machine made him feel like he had been inserted into a tube, and his heart began to pound, his breathing became rapid and shallow. Suddenly but calmly, the words "The Lord is my shepherd, I shall not want . . ." came into his mind, and he repeated the psalm over and over in his mind until his heartbeat slowed and his breathing calmed. The machine surrounding him seemed to open up, and he drifted on the comfortable mantra of the psalm. The comforting words and tunes of a memorized verse can make a real difference in facing fear and crisis throughout our lifetimes. They are part of the endowment passed to us as children by the people of the church.

Another endowment for our children, as we bless them, is our prayer for and with them. Prayer is a gift of safety, of belonging, and of grace. I remember clearly the image of my own daughters, Emily and Amanda, at about five and three years old, as they prayed before bedtime in a lengthy and heartfelt ritual that allowed them to end their day and to drift safely and securely to sleep. Many times when I have led the prayers of the people in worship, I have suggested that the congregation "cuddle up" and hold close the people they love during the prayers, so that children may feel an adult pray (or adults may feel a child pray!). Even the simple act of calling a child by name in prayer is part of this blessing, this endowment of belonging to a community of faith where we get occasional glimpses of the kindom of God.

In addition to blessing the children, we welcome children into the church because we are clearly told in the Gospel of Mark that whoever welcomes a child welcomes Jesus Christ, and whoever welcomes Jesus welcomes also God (Mark 9:36-37). Here Jesus has identified so closely with a child that he affirms his very presence in the child. How can we, as followers of Christ, not welcome the children? Like the word *blessing* with its dual meaning, *welcome* has more than one meaning. The context of its use usually dictates whether *welcome* means to appreciate, to greet, or to receive. I believe that the kindom of God, and the text in Mark 9, requires Christians to use all three meanings of the word *welcome*.

In what ways does our welcoming the children of our churches express its meaning of appreciation? This is where the most basic hospitality questions become important. This kind of welcome is shown through the physical condition of our worship settings, fellowship space, grounds, and classrooms. Have you ever walked into a church and known immediately that children are appreciated there? This is a place with signs at child-eye level, children's bulletins and other worship aids, nametags for children as well as adults, and so on. Recently a child at our church was so thrilled to find her nametag in the rack with all of the others that she sought me out to show me. She pointed out its place on the nametag rack, empty now that she was wearing it. It told her that we appreciate her. We know her name and respect her. She is welcome here. Most of all, it said, "Jacqueline, you belong here."

This borders on the second definition of *welcome*, which is "to greet." We welcome each child to our church by name and by inclusion in our ministries. Eight-year-old Rachel serves as an usher each week she is at our church. She is welcomed by the other ushers, as she takes her place among them in the long walk from narthex to altar. She is greeted by the smiles and looks of recognition from the parishioners as she takes the offering. She catches my eye at the altar, and smiles.

The third meaning of *welcome,* to which we must attend if we are to catch a glimpse of the kindom, is "to receive." Again, this shares some space with the other meanings, greeting and appreciating, but in the Christian church it is more than that. It is the welcome provided through baptism. It is, again, God calling each child by name and claiming that child as God's own.

So, we welcome children into the church in order to bless them. But the Bible has a lot more to say about the inclusion of children in the kindom. Throughout the Bible, God is the One who is the advocate for the widow and orphan, the least of these, the vulnerable.

The Old Testament specifically indicates the need for education of children (Proverbs 22:6, for instance), and a consistent theme throughout the Old Testament is the longing for a child. This is one indication of the value of children to the culture. Children of the Hebrew Scriptures were called by God (Samuel, Jeremiah) and protected and employed by God (David, Moses). In Matthew and Luke, the birth story of Jesus is vital. The birth

List the children of the Bible. What are their stories, and what do these stories mean for our ministries with children?

story of Jesus teaches us that nothing is greater than a child; in fact, our Christian story begins here. When Jesus was twelve he was found in the synagogue listening and asking questions. Those observing were amazed at his understanding, a lesson to those of us who fail to understand that we can learn from children. Perhaps I read with a bias, but I am unable to find reference in the Bible to any negative influence of a child, abuse of power by a child, or evil intent of a child. The Bible holds children in very high esteem. The Bible has included, welcomed, blessed, and lifted up the ministry of the child, with the child, for the child, and to the child.

Finally, I believe our understanding of God as a God of love requires bringing our children's ministries out of the basement. Again, consider the Hebrew Scripture references to protecting the least of these and, in the New Testament, Jesus' words that one must become like a child. Knowing that in the culture of Jesus' time, a child had no rights, no status, no privilege, why would Jesus require people to become like children? Because all it requires to be included in God's family is to be. "Jesus loves me, this I know" is a song sung and understood by every child in our churches. In the kindom of God, perhaps, there is no basement.

Chapter 2
The Body of Christ

*For just as the body is one and has many members, and
all the members of the body, though many, are one body,
so it is with Christ.*

1 Corinthians 12:12

Systems theory sounds like a complicated idea. In truth, it is a helpful tool for thinking about the function, purpose, and structure of an organization, such as the church. Whether we are talking about family systems or organizational systems, the basic premise behind this theory is that a system is composed of interdependent parts and a change in any one part will have an effect on the entire system.

In the last chapter, I argued that a primary hope for children's ministry is to bring about the kindom of God on earth. This vision pulls us into the future, compelling new ways of thinking and being. In 1 Corinthians 12:12-26, Paul gives us a clear metaphor for the church. We can view the church as a system, an interdependent group of parts (people, ministries, and so forth) working together toward a common vision. Using the body of Christ as a metaphor, we create a model for viewing ministries in the church. Following the biblical text, we are all, though many, a part of one body. The parts of the body that seem weaker are in fact "indispensable," those that are "less honorable" are clothed "with greater honor," and the parts we consider less respectable are shown greater respect. If one member suffers, so do all, and if one is honored, we all rejoice. Imagining your church as a body, what are the weaker parts and how are they indispensable?

What are the seemingly weak yet indispensable parts of your church body? What part do children play in the body's functions?

Often, children are viewed as weaker, as dependent and offering little contribution to the whole. In the kindom, children are indispensable, a vital contributing part of the body.

We all have stories from our ministries about this concept. I remember a child I will call Gwen in our Sunday classes who would be considered a weaker part of our community. She was in a wheelchair almost all of the time due to a debilitating muscular disease. Whenever we did presentations or even when the children's choir sang in worship, one of the other children would push her chair onto the stage or into the chancel so that she could participate. Her voice was often louder than the others and, just as often, way off key. Her lyrics were slurred and incomplete. Each time the children sang, Gwen's head moved from side to side, and her arms would beat against the chair to a rhythm only she could hear. But Gwen had great power in the community of that church. At the end of each piece of music, each child's part in the presentation, every Christmas carol, and each instrumental offering, Gwen would break into loud and enthusiastic applause. Her gratitude for the offerings of the group was so evident that it was contagious. It spread to the congregation and to the children each and every time. Gwen knew what more of us should know. The most important job in any presentation or musical offering was supporting and encouraging everyone who participated. As we included Gwen over the years, her enthusiasm and encouragement became highly important to the whole church. She is gone now. Her illness forced her into a different living situation, and the family moved to be close to her. For years after she left, she was remembered and missed at the end of every song by the children's choir and every presentation of the children's classes. She was one who seemed to be the weak one but was indispensable to the feeling of wholeness of the community.

What this story tells us about children's ministry as a whole is even more complicated and yet very simple. There is a place for all children and all adults in our ministry with, by, for, and to children. Furthermore, that place is vital for each child, and each child is crucial to the overall ministry. Finally, it is very much aligned with the gospel. Jesus said, "Let the little children come to me; do not stop them; for it is to such as these that the kingdom of God belongs" (Mark 10:14).

Looking again at 1 Corinthians 12:12-26 we see that Paul is using a systems approach to describe the church. That is, when we speak of the church as a body with many parts, which rely on each other and support each other, we are talking about a method for visualizing the church as an interdependent group of people, processes, functions, and activities that work together for a common goal. This common goal is often called the mission of the church.

Again, we turn to the Biblical text to define the mission of the church. Matthew 28:18-20 is pretty clear about that. Jesus appears to the disciples and tells them that all authority on earth and heaven has been given to him. In other words, nothing had more power than the words of Jesus at that moment and the disciples had better listen up. He said, "Go therefore and make disciples of all nations, baptizing them in the name of the Father and of the Son and of the Holy Spirit, and teaching them to obey everything that I have commanded you." This powerful text gives us a very clear mission: to make or form disciples. But we must also include in the mission statement some understanding of what these disciples are to do. Without such an understanding, the work of the church would end when disciples were sent out. According to both the Hebrew Scripture (Old Testament) and New Testament, what God requires of us is to feed the hungry, clothe the naked, and visit the prisoner (Matthew 25). We are required to provide "justice to the weak and the orphan," to "maintain the right of the lowly and the destitute," to "rescue the weak and the needy" (Psalm 82), and to do justice, love mercy, and walk humbly with God (Micah 6). Clearly, we are called to make disciples who will transform the world to approach the *kindom* of God.

Once we have agreed on a mission, forming disciples who will transform the world into the kindom, we begin to consider how to accomplish this. Our mission is the frame in which we place a picture or vision that will help us fulfill our mission. Our vision leads us forward into the future, helping us to recognize what our mission looks like when lived out. As we formulate a vision, again the Scriptures give us guidance. The Great Commandment tells us that we are to love God and love one another. The mission, making disciples, is the picture frame while the vision, loving God and each other, is the picture in the frame. We then develop goals and objectives that will help us create the picture in the frame, disciples who are recognized by the love of God and love of each other. Our objectives might be statements that consider how we go about teaching people to care for each other. How we articulate our goals and objectives is based on each church's context, culture, past experience, and tradition.

So the church is a system, an interdependent group of people and processes with mission and vision. Goals and objectives can be defined that help achieve the church's mission. Like a human body system, the church

> **List other visions which might be "framed" by the mission of making disciples.**

body is a group of interrelated systems, or subsystems. For example, the human body has a circulatory system and a digestive system. The vision of both systems is sustaining life. The circulatory system has a defined mission of transporting cellular nourishment and waste management. The mission of the digestive system also concerns nourishment, but this system performs a different set of tasks to accomplish it. The circulatory system and digestive system need each other to sustain life in a fully functional way. It is possible to artificially sustain life in the absence of parts of one or the other, but some parts of both systems need to be functioning in order for a body to survive.

And so it is with the church body. There are various subsystems that make up the church, each with the mission of making disciples who will transform the world. The various age group ministries of your church might be subsystems through which your church works. Or perhaps your subsystems are oriented more by ministry group (work area) or committee, such as worship, music, evangelism, or education. Probably you have both of these kinds of subsystems. Ministry with, by, for, and to children is a subsystem in the Christian church. The mission of children's ministries in every church is to make disciples who will transform the world into the kindom. Even in those churches where there are no children, parts of a system of children's ministries must exist according to our biblical mandates for ministry. For example, a church without children of its own will still reach into the community and serve children there, or it will still support worldwide mission and relief efforts for children.

A primary implication of this kind of thinking about the church is that these subsystems do not exist in isolation but are parts of the whole. Just as the circulatory system and digestive system are interdependent, so are children's ministries and older adult ministries, or music and worship. We want all parts to work together at all times, like the human body, for the greatest hope of achieving the mission.

We can all cite many examples of those times when our church subsystems didn't work together. A change in one subsystem created ripple effects that eventually created havoc or, minimally, much grumbling! Those of us who work in multiple-staff churches have plenty of examples of these ripple effects. Recently, we were working on a new pictorial directory, which required a space in the church for the photographer and salesperson to be set up for three weeks. They were put into Pierce Hall, our basement, until one of the pastors scheduled an art display and news conference, whereupon the photographers were moved onto the "ledge," two of the adult Sunday morning classrooms. This moved the Sunday classes into a large open area of Pierce Hall, affecting those people who hang around for coffee and fellowship instead of going to a class. These people went upstairs to the second floor to hang out near other classes, disturbing their lessons with conversations and laughter. What I heard first was a complaint from the teacher of a class on the second floor about the difficult time he was having teaching, and it took me some time to uncover the initial difficulty! I believe it's true that every one of these classes, activities, or ministries was "working" on the mission in

When have your church ministries (subsystems) worked independently of one another, causing an undesirable effect in another ministry area?

its own way. But they failed to remember that a small change in one part of the system had effects on the whole, and all were certainly affected by the small scheduling change. Children's ministry in our churches can be seen as a subsystem within our churches, but it doesn't exist without the other subsystems. We must be cognizant of the implications of changes to the system and to the other subsystems in the church. Again, children's ministries are an interdependent group of people, processes, functions, and activities that work together for a common aim, to make disciples who will transform the world.

This is not to say that all systems of children's ministry are alike. There are certain similarities, but each system of children's ministries may be unique to its own church. In my current setting, our system includes Sunday school, lots of advocacy work, family camping, intergenerational programming, nursery care, education on global issues, teacher education, and more. Not included in this system in this church setting are vacation Bible school, afterschool ministries, and other weekday children's ministry for school-aged children. I believe in and support these ministries in other settings, but we have a geographical disadvantage. The church is located in the heart of the city and a long drive from most of the members' homes. A couple of weeks ago I was doing an evaluation session with some of our little ones, and one of their biggest complaints about our church is the distance from home, traveled by train or car. This is a reminder of how interdependent our systems are. Transportation issues are also quite often vital to the functioning of several church systems at once.

Another way to look at the system of children's ministries in a church is to use the framework provided by the checklist in "A Church for All God's Children." This resource provides a comprehensive listing of ministries and actions of a church which are indicators of the church's inclusion of children's ministries. It was intended to be a guide for churches in assessing and upgrading their ministries in response to the Bishop's Initiative for

**How are the nine
listed areas
currently expressed
in your children's
ministry? How
might your
children's ministry
change if they were
more intentionally
expressed?**

Children and Poverty (see Chapter 1). It lists nine areas of ministry, each of which contains many programs and ministry areas:

• Educating the congregation about the needs of children and the poor.

• Making church facilities safe and welcoming for children and families.

• Reducing the risk of child abuse.

• Helping children grow as faithful disciples.

• Involving children in the life of the church.

• Reaching out to children in the community.

• Advocating for legislation and public policies that improve children's lives and lives of poor families.

• Relating to children around the world.

• Building administrative supports for ministry with children and the poor.

(From "A Church for All God's Children: Congregations Responding to the Needs of Children in the Church and Community," provided by the General Program Agencies of The United Methodist Church to the Bishops' Initiative on Children and Poverty, 1998.)

I have selected these components as an organizing schema for this book because they provide a comprehensive and holistic content for a system of children's ministries. Each of these areas of children's ministry could be seen as part of a vision that moves us toward fulfilling our mission of forming disciples to transform the world into the kindom of God. Each will look somewhat different in different churches, and each will be enhanced by a variety of objectives and goals, short-term and long-term, which provide the nuts and bolts of a church's ministry.

One simple system is a bike and rider. The two need each other in order to accomplish the mission of movement. In this system, one part cannot accomplish the mission without the other. However, the two together can accomplish something in a way neither could accomplish alone. The components of a comprehensive system of children's ministry listed above are like that simple system. Many can exist without the others, but the progress toward the vision of the kindom is enhanced by the existence and participation of all.

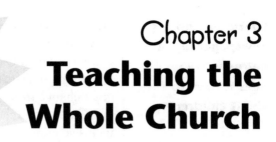

Chapter 3
Teaching the Whole Church

Come, let us go up to the mountain of the LORD,
to the house of the God of Jacob;
that he may teach us his ways
and that we may walk in his paths.

Isaiah 2:3

Whether you are a pastor, Christian educator, Sunday morning teacher, or parent, if you are beginning to think of creating or improving a holistic system of children's ministries in your church, a starting point is helping the congregation understand the needs of children. This is no easy task, as our society has some interesting attitudes toward children. We are very sensitive and concerned about the issues of when life begins and abortion, but as a whole our society demonstrates little regard for children. Check out the newspaper today. What does it tell you about children? If it is like the paper on the day I am writing this, you will see that children are consumers, crowd followers, not whole people, victims; materialistic, sweet, cute, innocent, guilty, violent, and expensive. While this is indeed a step ahead of the situation a century ago, when, for the most part, children weren't even in the newspapers, society still views children in a great variety of ways and doesn't assume responsibility for their well-being. This is one of those instances in which being the church is a great gift. As Christians, we have a biblical and theological mandate to care for the children, each of whom is precious to God. The church has been at the forefront of improving the lives of children. Our first task in educating the congregation

Check out today's newspaper or Internet news. What does it have to say about children?

about the needs of children is to reinforce this very basic premise of the Christian church. The church needs to be a safe sanctuary for children. Creating a holistic children's ministry requires a great change from the way things have always been in our churches to a new vision of an inclusive ministry for children where they, as smaller, weaker, and needier, are always safe.

I earlier described the "Church for All God's Children" checklist as offering a comprehensive listing of ministries and actions of a church which are indicators of the church's inclusion of children's ministries. It was intended to be a guide for churches in assessing and upgrading their ministries in response to the Bishop's Initiative on Children and Poverty. The first area listed, "Educating the Congregation," is defined as a teaching process with an outcome of sensitizing the congregation to the lives and needs of children so that the church might respond in just and compassionate ways. I believe our need for education goes beyond that. Education about the needs of children in our churches and in the world is the foundation of our ministries with, by, for, and to children. We need to know about the children in order to meet their basic faith needs. We need to know about them in order to set our priorities for ministry. Most importantly, we need to know the children of our churches and world so that we might love them with the church's whole heart. We need to know children in order to make disciples who bring about the kindom.

The need is great, and the issues are large and complex. In order to approach this in a more organized way, I suggest six objectives within this vision of educating the congregation:

- Reinforce the theology of children's ministries through all possible means in the church (sermon, story, classrooms, counseling, and so forth).
- Solicit help, both people and resources.
- Understand who your children are.
- Determine the church's vision for children's ministries.
- Understand how the congregation communicates and how decisions are made.
- Communicate with all church members, including children.

Let us look in more detail at each of these six objectives.

1. Reinforce the Theology of Children's Ministries Through All Possible Means in the Church.

Essential Resource: *Putting Children and Their Families First* **(see page 103)**

At all possible times and in all possible places, we should lift up the needs of children, give voice to the issues affecting children, and help people remember how much God loves each and every child. In our songs, in our sermons, and in the way we interact with each other, we must remind the congregation that Jesus loves the children. Our children's workers must reflect God's love and our parents must be helped to understand God's grace through the actions of their preschoolers. All of the help we recruit in our vacation Bible schools, in our nurseries, or in afterschool programs must re-present God's love to our children. Our older parishioners need to be constantly reminded of God's creating action in the new life of our nurseries as well as in our exuberant youth groups. Our clergy and laypeople alike must know and understand the Biblical mandate to care for our children and to keep them safe.

Think about the various groups of people in your church. How can you help them learn and remember the theological foundations of children's ministries? What factors work to assist in this process? What works against it?

2. Solicit Help.

Without well-trained, well-informed help, we cannot even begin a comprehensive ministry with, by, for, and to children. The work of the community is crucial to all we do in the church. A solitary voice rarely has the effect that a chorus of voices has. Two hands can do the work, but twenty can get it done in a timely way. Ten heads can produce ideas a single one would never imagine. Most importantly, each person who is involved in the work is validated and affirmed by the ministry, and each takes it into the world in different ways.

Getting help in your congregation is an ongoing task, and it is important to recognize this. Not everyone will be able or willing to help. But for some people, it will become an answer to prayer, the discovery of their calling. There is a woman in a suburban Chicago church who answered a conferencewide call for people to be trained to help churches develop policies and procedures to reduce the risk of child abuse. She became so energized by the training that she went on to become a district spokesperson and has helped organize major changes in her own church in children's ministries. She began to read Scripture in worship and to help lead in other ways, and she was recently licensed as a local pastor in our conference as she continues her discernment of God's call in her life.

Some other keys to getting help are:

- Start with a small, group task, a reason to bring a group together, perhaps an assessment of current ministries for children in your church.
- Enlist people for the amount of time they can give.
- Support people with information and gratitude.
- Keep other church staff and leadership informed.
- Keep records of your work.
- Remember that the risen Christ is at the heart of all you do.
- Pray about your efforts.

3. Understand Who Your Children Are.

Remember my story about Jacqueline and her nametag in Chapter 1 (page 13)? We know her name, her age, and other demographic information about her. We have an up-to-date database that tells all kinds of facts about her. But we also know that, as a seven-year-old, she is probably at a certain point in her faith development, and the whole congregation knows that she is apt to get up at least twice during worship to take a short walk out of the sanctuary for new colored markers or a restroom trip. We remind each other that she needs our smiles, our greetings, and, most of all, our time. We post pictures of her accomplishments in choir, class, and worship leadership. Every time we have a chance, we tell the congregation about our children. We share stories and joys and concerns in their growth.

We also know something about the children of the church today through generational theory. The current children in our churches are part of the "millennial" generation, a group with distinct characteristics and preferences. A short-term course in generational theory would be very helpful to your congregation. Of primary importance to the work of generational theorists in the church is the emphasis on finding ways to help this generation be disciples who will make a difference in the world.

There are other aspects of knowing the children that are not quite as easy. One is the understanding that the children in our community and world are also our children and our responsibility. This understanding can be fostered by making it a key thesis in sermons and classes for youth and adults. Participation in a Children's Sabbath (the Children's Defense Fund in Washington, D.C., prepares wonderful Children's Sabbath materials annually; see the resource list) and other worship services related to children's issues are also helpful in educating the congregation about the needs of children beyond their church doors. It may be beneficial to invite members of the community from various agencies and advocacy groups to teach short-term classes on their work or host a community information fair. The hope is that we will educate the congregation so that they will understand who our children are and can then respond through their ministries with grace and love.

4. Determine the Church's Vision for Children's Ministries.

Helping the congregation identify its vision for children's ministries and set priorities based on that vision is essential. Without strategic planning (or vision planning or whatever your church wants to call it) the awareness of the vastness of what could be done becomes overwhelming. Churches can become defeated by the magnitude of the issues or scattered across too many important issues in their ministry. It is helpful to determine a vision for three or four major areas of children's ministry each year and to build from there. For example, when I first started my ministry at Trinity UMC in Wilmette, Illinois, our primary vision was to build the Sunday school by empowering teachers and creating safe environments that were education-ally appropriate. It became clear that we needed to work on small pieces of even this vision, a little at a time, as we renovated physical space. We soon added issues of inclusion to our vision as more children began to participate. Over time, our vision changed completely, becoming still more inclusive, as we were able to move beyond the basic provision of ministry to children into ministry with, by, for, and to children in the world. Determining your vision is vital to educating the congregation, and it is a process that will change over time, in consideration of the needs of the church.

5. Understand How the Congregation Communicates and How Decisions Are Made.

Every church is different. A good place to begin to understand how your church communicates is by watching how current members (especially those who have been in the church a long time) communicate and by ask-ing them how they think the church communicates. Church staff usually have some valuable information to share on this topic, too.

It is also helpful to look at denominational resources, such as official rules for church functioning and publications of denominational bodies. In The United Methodist Church, for example, one can take a look at *The Book of Discipline of The United Methodist Church,* which suggests ways to organize a local church.

In any church, there are probably women's groups, men's groups, sin-gles' groups, and couples' groups, all of which have some knowledge to share and some understanding of how things get done in the church. There

List the ways that your church communicates with children.

is also some official body that makes policy and decisions that affect the entire church, such as a church council. Such a council would be the place for consideration of a vision for children's ministries as a priority of the church's ministry. Without a clear picture of how decisions (and hence, changes) are made, time will be wasted and efforts will go unnoticed.

6. Communicate With All Church Members, Including Children.

There are many ways to communicate with a congregation, and it is vital to continue to find new ways. We are a fast-paced society, used to information being blasted at us from all directions. Our children, the millennial generation, have been raised in an electronic and digital world that changes very quickly. Bulletin boards in the church facility still work for many congregations, but they must be supplemented with a website bulletin board. E-mail is common for families and children age four and sometimes younger. A church "chat" on Internet sites dedicated to exploring new ways of communication of church news and ministries would be very informative.

While there are many ways to communicate, two important points are: include children in communication and keep working on it! Think about the ways your congregation communicates and then brainstorm ways of using these communication methods to educate fellow members about children's ministry in your congregation.

This chapter doesn't have a list of items to tell the church. You need to determine what and how you will communicate in your own setting when you have decided what your vision for children's ministries will be. In my current church, our vision includes sensitizing the congregation to issues affecting children of our church and world. Legislative issues are part of the information that is communicated, through a variety of methods, as are current statistics on child poverty, health care, education, and hunger. We see this as one way we can begin to bring the kindom of God into our church.

Chapter 4

The First Three Things

*If any of you put a stumbling block before one of these
little ones who believe in me, it would be better for you if
a great millstone were fastened around your neck and
you were drowned in the depth of the sea.*

Matthew 18:6

Picture this: You are in an interview for a new job as a Christian educator. You really want it. The church is exciting, with many resources and possibilities. There is a newly remodeled office waiting for your books. The salary and benefit packages look good. There is potential for growth for the ministries you would lead as well as for yourself. Several people make up the interview team, and their semicircle of chairs faces your chair. The question: What are the first three things you would do in your work as minister with children in this place?

This actually happened to me. My first thought was to say I would pray, pray, and pray again, but these people wanted details. After a short time, I had the presence of mind to begin to talk about Abraham Maslow, a psychologist who proposed theories of human motivation. He said that every person has a hierarchy of needs, where basic needs of an individual must be met before needs higher in the hierarchy can be met. The base is physiological needs, such as food and water, followed by safety, belonging and love, self-esteem, and finally self-actualization. When all of the first four categories of needs are satisfied, then one can satisfy the needs of self-actualization, in which one achieves one's highest potential as a person. Over time, research has not verified that all needs of a given level of the hierarchy need to be met before one can progress, but at least some must be. So, the theory says, you must eat and breathe before you are too concerned about your safety, and you must feel relatively safe in order to love and be loved. In relation to a church, especially to the work of Christian education and children's ministries, this theory implies that we must be sure the basic needs of children are met before we can approach some of the more creative and self-giving goals of our faith. With Maslow's theory in mind, my mind's eye viewed the educational areas of the church, and without any further hesitation I said I would clean up the children's space and make it safe for children, then fill it with love. The church needed to meet these basic needs of children of all ages before we could move on to finding the right curriculum resources or reenergizing the annual Advent workshop.

It was a good answer. Not only did I get the job but I also followed the plan. It correlates with the second emphasis of "A Church for All God's Children," which is to make the church facilities safe and welcoming for children and for families. The primary issues involved are safety and hospitality. Making the church safe and welcoming requires a little time, an ability to discard that which is no longer usable or is unsafe, a knowledge of child development, and some very dedicated people.

Cleaning up the areas where children's ministries occur is not as easy as it sounds, but it is the beginning place for children's ministry. The best part of this is that it gives you time and an activity over a period of weeks or even months during which you can get to know a group of people in your church a lot better! Assemble a group and get to work. Set up an area where all cleaning tools are to be found (and returned). Find four large clean trash cans or boxes, and label them Keep, Discard, Ask, and Recycle. The Ask can is for those items that you need to consult others about before you discard or recycle them. For example, I nearly discarded a lovely but tattered banner that hangs in a classroom, but decided I had better wait and ask. I later found out it was made by the children of one of our most active workers who would have been very unhappy if it had been removed. Empty the cans or boxes after every work session. Throw away all toys and materials that are unusable due to missing parts, broken pieces, or unsafe characteristics. Ask one of your members to examine basic equipment—cribs, tables, chairs, large toys, and highchairs—to be sure they meet current child safety standards. Inventory your equipment, making a list of needs and items to be replaced. A church body that considers its children to be one of its most important parts will not be satisfied with unsafe equipment. Replacement cost is often cited as a reason for keeping outdated equipment. A child's injury or even death is a much higher cost to pay. Having fewer but safer items is a better choice than having many marginally safe items.

Essential Resource:
The First Three Years
(see page 103)

Cleaning and making your church safe for children go together. All old, toxic craft materials should be discarded and replaced with safer products. You may need to investigate the situation in your church regarding pest control and its safety. Other tasks include: covering electrical outlets, installing or testing fire and smoke alarms, checking and replacing the contents of first aid kits (being sure to include gloves for dealing with spills of body fluid, such as blood). Organize potentially dangerous supplies and equipment so that children cannot access them. Our teachers use razor-blade knives in the classrooms to cut tagboard, foamboard, and other materials. These knives are placed high on a shelf in a box called "administration," where the teachers can find and return them but the children cannot reach them. An even better choice would be to lock up these kinds of items.

All toys should be washed regularly and inspected for safety. Safety also means selecting items with the size and ability level appropriate for the age of the child who will use them. Manufacturers provide a general guideline. Check manufacturer's catalogs for the age guidelines of older toys or equipment that have lost their original labeling. If you know the brand of an item, you can also check the website or call the manufacturer. Such a call enables you to also find out about recalled toys. Perhaps someone on your team would be willing to take the job of keeping informed about toy recalls on an ongoing basis. It's an important issue for children, parents, and grandparents.

A disinfectant, gloves, and other cleaning supplies should be safely stored where your "cleaning task force" has access to them. Fabric toys that cannot be washed, such as many stuffed animals, should not be in the children's areas. Hats and other costumes should be regularly washed and sprayed with a lice-killing product. Be sure to read labels so that the products you use are used safely and effectively.

A word about "recycling." Recycling means actual transformation of materials into a newly usable product, such as the paper recycling being done in most churches today. But it also means donating usable items to charities or missions where people in need can use them. The key word here is *usable*. A charity does not want dolls with no heads or a rocking chair with no seat. I was told of a woman in the church who was saving her used tea bags to send to a mission overseas because they had only been used once! My grandmother, God bless her, used to cut the buttons off clothing before donating them to a charity. This was a frugal habit left from

Take an inventory
of your existing
church groups.
Which would be
willing to help in a
cleaning and safety
effort and in what
ways?

the Depression, but what she ended up giving away then had little value. Donate usable items.

Every floor, toilet, and corner should be cleaned, every window washed, and every curtain, rug, or drapery washed or dry-cleaned. A child (as well as a parent) entering a clean and organized space will know that you care and are trying to keep the children in your church as safe as possible. Additional safety considerations include many of the child-abuse prevention actions described in Chapter 5, but accessibility is also a safety and hospitality issue. Making your areas accessible for people with disabilities provides safe access as well as easier access. Many denominations and United Methodist annual conferences have guidelines, suggestions, or even personnel to help you achieve accessibility.

A church that is dedicated to bringing children's ministries out of the basement will have a variety of groups that are willing to assist in the efforts to make the church clean and safe for children's ministries. The trustees, for example, can examine their current insurance policies to check on coverage for bodily injury or liability coverage for volunteers and staff if a person is injured. Some insurance companies even discount premiums for certain safety actions, such as installing smoke detectors and fire extinguishers. Certain women's groups may have an interest in fundraising to assist in the replacement of outdated nursery equipment, or a social group might be willing to spend a Saturday morning repairing and cleaning up the playground. The parents' class might help develop a fire evacuation plan.

Bringing children's ministries out of the basement requires the involvement of the whole church in a number of different ways. Cleaning and making a church safe are two of the first three things. The involvement of the whole church begins to fill it with genuine and hospitable love for the children, the third of the first three things. When it is clean, organized, and safe, many people can begin to make the church welcoming for children by ensuring that rooms specifically for the children (classrooms, nursery, and so forth) are visually stimulating and bright. Directional signs with pictures should be posted at child eye level, and there should be step stools by drinking fountains and by other adult-sized equipment that may be used by children. We have a step stool in our chancel area, ready for use at either the pulpit or the lectern when children read or speak. If your church has a media center or library, stock it with a good supply of children's books and tapes that are consistent with your church's beliefs. Dare to be the church by being different from the rest of the world by finding church-related and

Bible-based books and toys, not secular ones. I so often wonder why our church preschool dress-up areas, for example, are filled with cowboy costumes and princess dresses. Why not choir robes and clerical stoles, hymnals, a chalice and paten?

Describe people in your past who were important to you as teachers and leaders in the church or community. What were their major personality attributes? What did they have in common?

Filling the spaces in the church with love for children includes advocacy. Speaking and doing on behalf of children is a way to demonstrate the church's love. Another very important step to filling the children's areas, in particular, with love is to recruit teachers, mentors, and caregivers who love children. Can you remember someone in the church or community when you were a child who shared God's love with you? Love for children should be the primary characteristic you look for in your "workers" in children's ministries, but there are many more. Look for people with existing skills or talents that you can build upon. Look for enthusiasm and appreciation for children. Weekday schoolteachers, for example, may not want to spend every Sunday morning teaching children, but they may be very interested in being confirmation mentors, nursery caregivers, or substitute teachers. They may also have much knowledge to share in teacher education and skill training on a quarterly or annual basis.

Recruitment of workers requires getting to know the people of the church and constantly searching for ways they might be involved with children's ministries. This is an everyday job, not an annual teacher recruitment marathon. At one church I served there was a men's group called the "Monday Morning Quarterbacks" that met every Monday at about 9:30 A.M. for coffee and conversation. They critiqued the Sunday services and classes and shared their lives with one another. Getting my own cup of coffee one morning, I dropped in to say hello and shared plans for our upcoming vacation Bible school. It was to be a marketplace approach, where our learning centered around a creatively built "town" from A.D. 29 of borrowed Boy Scout tents and card-table artisan centers. The center of the artisan market was a well, which was integral to several of the stories we would share with the children. What might I use for a well, I wondered? They immediately volunteered, and for years, our VBS had a wonderful brown tiled well, complete with a sign that said "500 feet deep" and a bucket on a rope. I "recruited" these men through an everyday effort to involve the people of the church in children's ministries.

There are many helpful resources on recruitment. In fact, it is such a fundamental part of children's ministries that nearly every children's ministry periodical has an occasional article on it and nearly every book has a chapter devoted to it.

Of the utmost importance is defining the task you wish to be done by a volunteer before you begin to recruit! Job descriptions help people know what they are expected to do and also help you identify possible areas where additional training needs to be done. The success of any recruitment effort hinges on current and previous support of the volunteers. This may relate to the work of a committee or ministry group in a church as well as to individuals. The pastor, for example, should take a role in this, thanking people and checking with them on their work with the children. Pastors can also lift up the importance of such ministry, and all ministries with children, in sermons and classes. Support should also come in the forms of the availability of substitutes for teaching and other ministries, observation of and feedback on the volunteer's ministry, interest in the volunteer as a person, and dependable provision of needed supplies, resources, and equipment. Support is also personal, taking an interest in the work, lives, and ministries of the volunteers, helping them through rough times and celebrating with them in their joyous times. And don't forget to check references and backgrounds of all volunteers. You may save a child's life.

An interesting recruiting idea that I am learning more about in my current ministry is a "wagon-wheel" approach to volunteer recruitment. There is a central group of people who act as the placement agency for all of the church's volunteers. People are assigned to work projects and task forces, based on their skills and passions, for relatively short terms. When a project is finished, the volunteers return to the "pool" to await the next assignment. This kind of approach works well with short-term projects in children's ministry. It can create a highly motivated group of workers for each task and keep people from being burned out, ignored, or stuck in committee work for which they aren't well suited.

Filling a church with love also requires a churchwide understanding of the issue of discipline of children. Each church should have a written policy stating how children in the ministries of the church are disciplined, and the policy should be reviewed often. My church's current policy is quite simple, stating that after "repeated warnings" a child will be asked to take a time-out. If that doesn't work, the child will spend time away from the group with a different adult. Finally, a parent is notified if the child continues to be disruptive. Teachers and children's leaders have a lot of room within that policy regarding the number of times a child can be "disruptive," what is offensive, and how long the time-out will be. The policy is written and sent to every family at the beginning of the year and is available in the classrooms at all times. In most classroom situations, the teachers also form a covenant of behavior with the students, so that they know what the expectations of behavior are. Forming a covenant or even sharing a list of rules helps the children feel as though they have had some input into the formation of the group. Rather than being punitive, it builds a group identity. Physical discipline is not allowed at our church (and should not be allowed in any church), and the teachers and others who work with children sign a statement agreeing to that when they apply to become volunteers in our children's ministries.

Clarifying the basics of discipline with the teachers and leaders will help them be more successful in all of their efforts. Teachers and leaders should help the children understand that there are natural consequences to actions. For example, if a child refuses to share the group's craft supplies, then the child cannot participate in that craft. If he or she breaks the crayons intentionally, the crayons will be put away. Other simple "rules" to keep in mind are never allowing the children to be alone; including time for movement and breaks as well as lessons and small motor activity; knowing how to get help when in an emergency; and having well-planned lessons and activities that will keep the children's attention and give them choices of activities.

So, the first three things I suggest are to clean, make safe, and fill with love. They can't happen in an exact order, nor can they happen in isolation. Further, you can't do it without the help of many people in your church who care about your children's ministries. It seems a little overwhelming at first, but you can begin in one place in the church, perhaps the nursery or the youth rooms, and move out from there. Or begin with one person who will work with you or a team in one space. Enthusiasm coupled with the church's visions will fuel your efforts quickly.

Filling the church with love is an attitude toward the church that says all people can be a part of our children's ministries in one way or another and each will serve according to existing skills, talents, and willingness to learn new ways of reaching and teaching children. There are, of course, some safety considerations. This attitude of love is a basic characteristic of all who follow Jesus as disciples and who are growing in discipleship even as they help form new disciples.

Chapter 5

Not in My Church

For this child I prayed; and the LORD has granted me the petition that I made to him. Therefore I have lent him to the LORD; as long as he lives, he is given to the LORD.

1 Samuel 1:27

It has become such a common story that people outside of the affected church are hardly shocked by it. A child is molested in the church bathroom by a trusted church-school worker. An infant is inappropriately fondled in the nursery by a teenage caregiver. A mentor at the church-housed tutoring program is charged with repeated inappropriate sexual behaviors with many children over a long period of time. A church daycare worker is discovered showing pornographic materials to the children for whom she cares. Each of these stories was in our local news in the past year. In fact, these stories are so common that I can even write them out in real words without flinching at the content as I would have done a few years ago.

But people in the affected church, the one where any of these crimes may have been committed, are shocked and fearful. "It can't happen here," they say. "Not in my church. My church is a place of safety and sanctuary." It shouldn't happen here, friends, but it does. No place in our modern and violent society will ever be completely safe from child abuse, sexual, physical, or emotional. In 1 Samuel 1:27, Hannah devoted her son, Samuel, to God's work. She did so out of trust that the house of worship was a safe and healthy place for him, just as our contemporary parents trust that our

Essential Resource:
Safe Sanctuaries:
Reducing the Risk of
Child Abuse in the
Church
(see page 104)

churches are safe and healthy places for their children. But this is no longer true, if, indeed, it ever was.

Further, as people who recognize children as a vital part of the body of Christ, we should be outraged at child abuse in any form, in any place. It not only shouldn't happen here, in the church, it shouldn't happen anywhere.

Correlating with the emphasis in "A Church for All God's Children," this chapter is about how we can begin to reduce the risk of child abuse in our churches. I believe this is one of the most important visions for children's ministry and am actively involved in "Safe Sanctuaries" training for conference and local church leadership.

The Safe Sanctuaries effort is another aspect of making our churches safe for children and is a mandate of our General Conference, the only body that can speak for The United Methodist Church. Check your denomination's polity for information on required efforts in this area for your local church.

You may also wish to check with your insurance carrier regarding this issue, as some companies require child-abuse policies and procedures to be in place before adequate coverage is issued. This, in fact, has been one of the driving forces behind attentiveness to the entire issue. Sadly, in many cases, the main concern hasn't been the well-being of the children but rather the cost of possible legal action in such cases. There is no doubt that judgments against churches in child-abuse cases have been devastating to individual churches, pastors, and other staff members. In my work with the Safe Sanctuaries workshops, I was told of a church that had to close its doors because of a judgment against the church.

The theology of children's ministry also requires us to ensure a safe sanctuary. Look at the hymns we sing about children. For example, consider "Away in a Manger," a well-known hymn sung by children and adults alike. It clearly describes the safety and security of a relationship with Jesus, especially the phrase "Be near me, Lord Jesus, I ask thee to stay close by me forever, and love me, I pray; bless all the dear children in thy tender care." At a child's baptism the congregation promises to care for and love the child. We are told over and over again in Scripture to care for and protect those who cannot protect and care for themselves. Our mandate is to protect each child as best we can from any form of abuse, and that especially includes abuse within our own ministries and programs.

In order to begin to ensure a safe sanctuary, we must take several steps:
 • Learn about the problem.

 • Develop, utilize, and continually evaluate and update a policy that outlines basic procedures for safety and for dealing with incidents in the church.

- Train all people who minister with children in the policies and procedures approved by our church.
- Educate children on prevention, abuse awareness, and self-protection.
- Inform and educate parents and guardians on prevention and awareness issues.

What human resources are available in your congregation to help develop and implement policies and procedures that will reduce the risk of child abuse?

- Outline possible steps for healing that the congregation will implement if an incident occurs in the church or community.

Additional resources are available to help you address these six issues (see pages 103-5). Also each community and church probably has a wealth of human resources that can be used to help address these issues. Your insurance company may be helpful in providing resources to your church. You may wish to recruit a task force or committee to work on all or parts, but it is vital to inform the entire congregation of progress and to work within your church's structure to approve congregationally the policies and procedures. In addition, you may find out that your conference, district, cluster, or area governance bodies have policies or requirements regarding these issues, so you would have that additional input.

In 1996 the General Conference of The United Methodist Church passed a resolution calling on local churches to develop policies and procedures to reduce the risk of child abuse. Various agencies of the church, including the General Board of Discipleship, the General Council on Finance and Administration, the General Commission on the Status and Role of Women, and the General Board of Global Ministries (National and Women's Divisions), provide resources that can be helpful as you develop these policies. In addition many annual conferences provide training or have trainers who can assist local churches. Other churches in your area may have already done some important and helpful work that can assist you in this task.

In teaching the church and parents about the problem, it is important to develop an understanding of the five kinds of abuse (physical abuse, emotional abuse, neglect, sexual abuse, and ritual abuse) and to know the indicators of each. Signs include changes in behavior, unexplained injuries, depression, untreated medical conditions, extremes of behavior, fear of adults, and more. In the church, there may be particular signs, such as fear of or hostility toward a specific teacher or caregiver, or a change in attitude toward attendance, nightmares, dreams which depict a church worker as frightening, or artwork that depicts the same. Children who have been ritually abused may be afraid of persons in robes or of ministers.

Training people who work with children to recognize the signs of abuse goes hand in hand with educating the entire congregation: People who work closely with the children, however, should be especially aware of changes in a child's behavior as an additional indicator. It is also important to have a policy in place that helps a teacher or worker know what to do if he or she suspects child abuse may be occurring in the home or another setting.

Child abuse in the church has many victims, including the child and family, the congregation and leadership, and the family of the accused abuser. In her workshops on Safe Sanctuaries, Joy Melton tells about a teacher she knows who was perplexed one Sunday when she gave one of her routine hugs to a child and he began to scream that she was hurting him. The teacher looked up to see the child's father in the doorway aiming a video camera at the two of them, obviously staging an "incident." The case, as obvious as it was, was thrown out of court, but the incident did an incredible amount of damage. It started church rumors about the teacher and was a terrible, hurtful experience for all involved. It cost the teacher and the church in terms of time, money, and reputation. For us, in this holistic children's ministry we are building, it points out the care we must take as we deal with this issue in our churches. Not all accusations are founded on fact. Some are misunderstandings, some are just plain lies. The alleged abuser could, in fact, be a victim.

The best approach to the whole issue is, again, to try to take the steps necessary to prevent child abuse from occurring in your church in the first place. Education and training are two steps, and a third is to develop, utilize, and continually update a policy that outlines basic procedures for safety. The policy should be written and voted on by the church and published for all to read. This will not only be a barrier to possible abusers but will also reassure parents and guardians. The policy should clearly state that child abuse in the church is unacceptable and should outline procedures for prevention as well as response.

Many churches' policies include a two-nonrelated-adult rule, which states that one adult will not be left alone with children. This also protects the adults against situations like the episode previously mentioned.

Screening of workers, caregivers, and teachers is also an important preventive step, and many insurance companies are now making it easier to do official background checks by tying discounted rates for such checks to their policies. Screening minimally includes application forms, interviews, and reference checks. In my current church, people cannot work with the children (as a leader or caregiver) unless they have been members of the church for at least six months. For protection of both children and volunteers, you may wish to have a minimum age requirement for workers, such as eighteen, and not allow anyone to work with children who isn't at least five years older than the oldest child.

Another protective response to this issue is to review your church's and the staff's insurance protection and update it to include coverage for allegations of sexual and physical abuse.

Other basic safety procedures include an open-door policy or windows in the doors; hall monitors and other adults who roam from room to room without a schedule; and procedures for signing in and out of areas and for transporting children from one area of the church to another.

A list of response procedures should clearly define the protection of the victim as the immediate concern, emphasize confidentiality issues, and spell out who should be informed by whom. It is important to have the name or position of someone who is not a staff member on the list in case a staff person is involved. In our church, the chair of our staff/parish personnel committee may be informed in such cases.

Finally, it is important to regularly review and update your policies and procedures. For example, listing a name or position on the reporting procedure is not helpful if the person is no longer with the church or position titles have changed.

Use age-appropriate curriculum resources for children on prevention, abuse awareness, and self-protection. These can be used in many settings, such as family retreats, vacation Bible school, summer classes, and so forth.

Informing and educating parents and guardians on prevention and awareness issues results in at least two outcomes. It assures parents of the safety of your church and gives them a basic understanding of the issue should their child be abused in another setting. Such education can be accomplished as the entire congregation is being educated, but parent groups can be highly effective small groups for learning and support. (For ease, I use only the word *parent,* but I mean a more inclusive group, including guardians and other caretakers.) A special parents' class on abuse issues may become the guiding task force that authors your church's policies and procedures. Don't underestimate the commitment and power of grandparents on this issue, too! Another benefit to the church from parent education classes may be the possibility of including the wider community in these classes, an opportunity for evangelism and ecumenical sharing of leadership resources.

A final yet life-giving step in your process toward creating a sanctuary safe from child abuse is to begin to outline possible steps toward healing in case an incident occurs in the church or community. How would you and your church respond? What avenues would you open for the healing power of the Holy Spirit in your church family? How would you talk about the case, how would the alleged victims and abusers be treated? Certainly, until an incident, true or false, occurs you will not know exactly how to respond, but it will be helpful to the entire church if this is discussed generically before it happens.

This chapter has been focused on preventing child sexual and physical abuse in our churches, but there are many more safety issues to consider in children's ministry. Safe physical spaces and toys were covered in the last chapter, and the need for a fire evacuation plan was mentioned. In addition to those, and depending on where your church is located, you will want to have a weather emergency plan. In Windom, where I grew up, the summers were full of warnings of tornadoes, and other areas have even more severe storms. A weather plan will differ from a fire evacuation plan, as the children would be taken to a safe place within the church. Ironically for this book, it may be the basement! Some churches are also formulating a violence response plan in the light of recent gun violence in our churches and schools. At the heart of all of this is the mandate to keep the children safe.

This is not an easy topic for churches. You may, as I have, come up against some very powerful opposition to some of the changes recommended. It is essential to educate the staff and congregation in such a way that they will settle for nothing less than the protection of the children. This is sometimes risky and almost always difficult, but the mandate is clear. There are a number of excellent resources suggested in Appendix B (see pages 103-5) that will help you to talk about these issues in your congregation and to develop appropriate policies and procedures.

Bad things happen to good churches and to good pastors in churches. And bad things happen to children, and they happen in our churches. We must do all we can to prevent child abuse in our churches, as we work to bring about the kindom in our midst.

Chapter 6
Growing as Disciples

Go therefore and make disciples of all nations, baptizing them in the name of the Father and of the Son and of the Holy Spirit, and teaching them to obey everything that I have commanded you.

Matthew 28:19-20

A kindergarten Sunday school teacher I know was observing her classroom of children while they drew. As she got to one little girl who was working diligently, she asked the child to tell her about the drawing. "I'm drawing God," she said. "But no one knows what God looks like!" exclaimed the teacher. The girl kept right on drawing. "They will when I finish this," she confidently said. This story brings up two underlying assumptions of this chapter:

1. Children have ideas about God because they are spiritual beings who are in relationship with God, and
2. A child's understanding of God and of his or her relationship with God changes over time as the child grows and matures.

This is probably the heart of this book, because it places the developmental needs of children in the context of the church system. It relates to the fourth emphasis of "A Church for All God's Children"—helping children to grow as faithful disciples.

Faith development is linked to all aspects of human development. Children are not little adults but are different and have different capabilities and ways of understanding. The mission of the church, articulated in Chapter 1, is to form disciples who will transform the world into the kindom of

God. The process of disciple formation begins before birth, with prenatal parent education and services, and continues until death. Some may argue that it actually begins long before a child is born, with the faith life of a child's ancestors, which is passed from one generation to the next in the way lives are led and in stories that are told. Childhood is a period of very rapid change and growth, including physical, mental or cognitive, emotional, moral, spiritual, and social development. We have a unique opportunity through the community of faith to encourage faith development as well as all other forms of development. Further, the church's understanding of child development allows for good utilization and planning of everything from the physical space to inclusion in worship services.

If we assume that children think, learn, and relate to the world in the same way adults do, we miss important opportunities to help children grow in faith, as well as opportunities to learn from children. One creative Sunday school teacher I know once asked the third grade class to write about what God does and how God is with us in the world. These turned out to be wonderful essays, illustrated with marvelous creative pictures. Their responses included ideas such as:

- God makes babies, which is pretty easy because they are smaller than us and can't do anything.

- God sees everything and hears everything and is everywhere, which keeps God pretty busy.

- Going to church on Sunday makes God happy and if there's anybody you want to make happy, it's God.

- If you don't believe in God you will be very lonely because your parents can't go everywhere with you and God can.

- God makes you feel better when the big kids make fun of you, and gives you special powers to do good things.

- God is with you all the time, even when you get lost on the way home from school because you went to the store first or when you get sick because you ate too much candy from the store.

- God sleeps with you, which you know because it feels so warm and safe under the covers.

People who are educated in child development would probably know that these ideas came from eight-year-olds, not six-year-olds or twelve-year-olds. They would know that an average child of eight is physically growing steadily, is acquiring skills quickly, and likes to participate. They would know that reasoning and discussing concerns are growing and practiced skills, that good memories are a basis for the child's actions, and that an

eight-year-old has a clear sense of right and
wrong. They would understand the child's faith
development and see in those sentences about
God a child who is most likely beginning to
move from a very self-centered way of understanding God to a more societal or communal
understanding. There is still a sense that "good"
people are blessed but not "bad" people, and
yet the children's ideas indicate that they have
questioned and struggled with some very important issues. There is an indication of awareness

Describe a child you know. What does the child think about God and the church? If you don't know, ask the child to describe God in words or pictures.

of violence and uncertainty, but also an underlying attitude of self-confidence
and hope for increased independence.

So what does knowledge of human development mean in relation to how
we include children in the ministries of the church? Obviously, in the light
of physical knowledge, it means having size-appropriate furniture and equipment in the classroom areas as well as any other places in the church where
children will likely spend time. What does this say about your sanctuary?
Can children see over the pew in front of them or could the sanctuary use
some booster seats? I know a church that provides rocking chairs in the
sanctuary. I imagine these chairs have made a difference for people in several age groups! Take a field trip, either in your mind or physically, to a
children's area in your church. Can you tell from its furnishings and supplies what age group it is intended for? If it is an intergenerational space,
what provisions are made for multiple age groups?

Understanding developmental differences also helps you decide how you
will reach people with different activities. For example, some churches have
an intergenerational Sunday school. The time together at church is filled
with learning that all ages can do together, including music, worship, and
craft and service activities. More age-level-specific activities are then provided to be done independently (or with parent help) at home.

Other churches have regular weekly dinners followed by learning activities. They spend time together as a large group, eating, singing, and getting
an overview of a theme for the evening, and then split into groups to work
on different activities ranging from art projects (older children) to lectures
(adults) to small group discussions (youth) to games (younger children).
Understanding how the various age groups learn and understand allows
you to appropriately staff, organize, and facilitate ministries so that everyone will gain the most.

In church classrooms, teachers need to be aware of developmental differences, too. In a preschool class, for example, the teachers need to know

How might you incorporate different ways of learning in your worship services?

what preschoolers are capable of doing (such as using scissors or putting together puzzles), how they get along together, how they understand about God, and how they understand prayer.

In addition to developmental differences, different people learn in different ways. We must be aware of the different ways in which people learn if we want to be able to reach everyone. For example, three important ways of learning are visual, auditory, and kinesthetic (related to physical movement). In learning situations, it is important to include all three ways of learning so that every child has the opportunity to learn in a way that is meaningful for him or her. For example, a story may be seen in pictures or video, it may be heard in the teacher's voice or in the children's retelling of it, and it may then be acted out in drama or with puppets. These three may occur together or individually.

Continuing to learn about the children they work with and using curriculum resources that are based on sound developmental and learning theory will enable teachers to enjoy a safe, effective, and fun time with the children. There are a wide variety of curriculum resources available for churches to use. In addition to examining the developmental appropriateness and the number of learning styles incorporated into the curriculum, there are many other questions to consider as you select resources. Questions to ask include:

- How are different cultures and races depicted in the resource?
- How are children with disabilities depicted in the resource?
- What images of God are used in this resource and are these images consistent with your church's understanding of God's nature?
- How is the Bible used in the resource?
- How will this resource help children be formed into disciples?
- Are a variety of learning styles used?
- Is there a clear structure or pattern to each lesson?
- Does the resource encourage learners to examine their own lives in the light of new learning or to make a behavioral change in the way they live?
- Can your church afford this resource?
- Are the beliefs expressed consistent with those of your church? (This is an extremely important question to ask if you are not

using curriculum resources approved by your denomination.)

- Does the teacher's guide provide adequate direction?
- Does the teacher's guide help the teachers to understand age-level characteristics and capabilities?
- How does the curriculum resource promote faith sharing in the home?
- Does the curriculum involve children in mission and ministry within and beyond the local church?
- What supplemental resources and supplies need to be purchased or located in order for you to use the resource effectively?
- What space and equipment will be needed to effectively use this resource? Is it available?
- How does the resource recycle or reuse supplies?

Make a list of criteria you would use in selecting resources. Review it and update it on a regular basis.

Helping children grow as disciples is an awesome task, and selecting appropriate resources and understanding human development and learning styles is important as we try to create a holistic approach to children's ministry. Nearly all curriculum resources, however, will need to be adapted to meet the needs of your particular situation. It is also important to keep in mind that whenever we categorize children or adults into groups that have certain abilities or understandings, we are making a generalization. We must remember that no child ever completely fits such a generalization, and individual needs and differences always exist.

Theorists have only begun to understand differences among cultural groups and even between the genders. These differences affect the way people develop and learn. We must use the work of developmentalists and those in related fields to assist in our task of forming disciples in the church, always seeing the individual child first. When I was in seminary, beginning to learn some of these ideas, I was told that young children do not understand symbols. They aren't, I heard, capable of the abstract thinking it requires to give meaning to a symbol. I was blessed at that time to spend much of my "free" time caring for my three children, three-year-old Amanda, five-year-old Emily, and nine-year-old David. One day I was also watching Amanda's friend, Trevor, and I decided to test the symbol theory I had read. I showed them my necklace, a cross, and asked what it was. None of them told me it was a necklace! Trevor said it was a "T for Trevor." Amanda said it was on the top of the church. Emily told me it

How does your church help families strengthen the home as a place of faith formation?

was a cross. And David said it meant "to remember where Jesus died." I think they all understood the symbol, but certainly at levels appropriate to their ages and experience.

To create an effective system for children's ministries we must continually examine the existing methods of forming disciples in the church and make changes constantly to accommodate new information, theories, and needs of individual children.

Successfully helping children to grow as disciples in the church means that leaders and teachers recognize that while not all children are the same, they must all be treated without bias. Furthermore, they are loved equally by God. One of the best gifts of my current church is the ethnic and cultural diversity of our children. Culture and traditions are shared each week in various ways as the children enter into the lessons and activities of the church. The preschool pretend kitchen has play foods from many traditions, and the children talk freely about their similarities and differences. This rich diversity is one reason people choose to come to our church. As children's leaders, we talk about meeting the needs of children of diverse backgrounds.

We also talk about gender bias, another kind of discrimination that we, as people who work with the children, often display without even knowing it. When we expect girls or boys to act in a certain way because of gender we are being biased. Some teachers, for example, might say that boys are inattentive and much more physical in their learning styles. While this might be true of some boys, it is also true of some girls and is not true of all boys or all girls. When we participate in gender bias, we are unfair in our expectations about how children will behave and how they will respond. Sometimes, gender bias is exhibited in the amount of positive or negative attention we give one gender over the other or the tasks we assign to them. For example, there was a first grade teacher in one of my churches who seemed to always require the girls to clean up, while the boys huddled around the classroom door, waiting for their parents. Part of the solution is to be aware of bias. Asking someone to observe your class will help you see if your leadership of children is gender biased. Once you are aware of your actions, you can consciously try to avoid bias.

Growing as disciples requires more than participating in church school and other ministries within the church. In a holistic approach to children's ministry, we recognize the home as one of the primary places where faith is formed and look for intentional ways to encourage faith sharing in the home. A very new tie between church and home is the development of church websites with bulletin boards where children can communicate with each other and with pastors and teachers.

We also help children to grow as disciples when we help them become involved in acts of compassion and justice, both in and beyond the church. Compassion and justice are both parts of being in ministry. Imagine you are standing by a river and injured people are floating by. Pulling the people out of the river and tending to their injuries are acts of compassion. When you walk upriver to find out why people are being injured and stop the people from being injured, you have accomplished an act of justice.

As a church, we must participate in both compassion and justice ministries with our children. They are capable of both, and both will facilitate their journeys as disciples of Jesus Christ who will transform the world into the kindom of God.

Stewardship is another part of discipleship. Children learn about stewardship through personal example, through participation in offerings at worship and other times, and through participation in the financial drives of the church. For example, children might save pennies to add to pledges for a new capital fund drive or help wash cars to support the youth group. Care of the earth's resources is certainly an important aspect of stewardship and is another area where the adults of the church can have great influence on how children understand stewardship. Does your church recycle cans, paper, and other materials? How can children help? Some churches plan environmental mission trips each summer that combine a work project with a family camping trip. The trip helps children and adults express their discipleship in new ways. Other churches participate in community clean-up efforts, sponsor recycling projects, or sponsor thrift stores that encourage the reuse of items. The possibilities are endless. They are an exciting part of a holistic children's ministry and are concrete illustrations of what it means to transform the world as disciples of Jesus Christ.

While appropriate curriculum resources, equipment, and facilities are significant when creating a holistic children's ministry, the most important ingredient is the faithful witness of "seasoned" disciples who serve as examples, teachers, mentors, and friends to our younger disciples. We have long known the value of such mentors with youth in confirmation journeys, and many community groups use mentors to reach and guide troubled or underserved youth. What would happen, I wonder, if a church were to assign (unrelated) mentors to every child each year, people who would take the time to talk to the children, be with them in classes, escort them in halls, sit near them in worship, and stand by them at fellowship time?

I believe that adults who take seriously the role they play as a model of Christian discipleship for children are more intentional about their own discipleship! Adults who are involved in the lives of children are a vital part of their growth into faithful adult disciples.

Helping children grow as disciples of Jesus Christ who will transform the world to achieve the kindom of God is a huge responsibility and a responsibility of the whole church. We must be intentional and reflective, constantly examining and evaluating our ministries, and we must remember, at all times, that God is alongside us. Hopefully, as we attend to this awesome task in the ways outlined in this chapter, we will keep our children aware of the presence of God, loving them and caring for them in all situations. Then in response to that knowledge of God's love, our children will share that love as disciples in the world.

Children's sermon

trying a new thing
Sometimes scary
feel unprepared
or don't know
enough

*give it a try

48

Chapter 7
And a Child Shall Lead

The wolf shall live with the lamb,
the leopard shall lie down with the kid,
the calf and the lion and the fatling together,
and a little child shall lead them.

Isaiah 11:6

I was getting ready to write this today, listening to National Public Radio while walking to an exercise video without sound. The radio station was in the middle of a pledge drive. My thoughts were half on the broadcast, and half on this chapter, when my attention totally turned to the radio. A child named Danny, age twelve, was on the line, promising to send in his five dollars to support the station. He said he liked the morning programs and thought he should do his part to pay for them. He said he knew five dollars wasn't much but was probably like fifty dollars to most adults, so he was sending it to the station. The commentator thanked Danny and said, "A child shall lead." I continued my walking and silently thanked the commentator for helping me see yet another way children lead us every day. Danny led as an example of good stewardship, but more importantly, he was saying very clearly that he is an integral member of the community.

Children lead us into participation in the community of Christ, the church. They lead us with their examples of stewardship, spirituality, and more. They lead us in discipleship in the church and world. Sometimes leadership means being at the front of a group, being in the spotlight, urging others to follow, like Moses. It can also mean providing an example or model from within the ranks of ordinary life of one who leads us to an awareness of everyday priorities, like Mary of Bethany (Luke 10:38-42). Either kind of leadership is impossible for children if they are left out of the life of the community.

In a holistic children's ministry, children are involved in the life of the whole church, not always segregated by age or sent to children's classrooms or nurseries. "A Church for All God's Children" calls this leadership function the inclusion of children in the life of the church, with the goal of "re-ordering congregational life in ways that recognize and involve children and youth as full participants" ("A Church for All God's Children" checklist, page 3). There are many areas where children can be included in the full life of the church, but the primary areas of inclusion, at least in my experience, are worship, education, pastoral care, evangelism, and mission.

Worship

One of the most important areas of the life of a disciple is worship. Including children in worship in ways that help them grow in faith is a challenge to worship planners and leaders. It must be intentional and grounded theologically and developmentally. We must consider our expectations of and from the children as we include them. For example, we may expect that they will make a little noise from time to time, and we hope that they will contribute some noise to unison prayers they may know or to psalms of praise. Regular involvement in worship requires us to do some creative thinking each time we plan it.

Children must be welcomed to worship and encouraged to participate in all parts of it. Include children's songs that they have learned in classes or in choir as part of the service. Use an advent candle lighting carol that is learned in the Family Advent workshop and is repeated each week for the four weeks of Advent. Encourage children to lead worship as liturgists, ushers, greeters, acolytes, communion servers, and more. Children can be included in training events for liturgists, creating an intergenerational opportunity for learning.

All God's children must be included in the sacrament of communion, and I am often surprised at the depths of a child's understanding of the sacrament. When my daughter Amanda was four, I asked her if she wanted to go up to take communion with me during a worship service. She enthusiastically said, "Yes! Jesus is there!" That may not be an "adult" understanding of the theology of Holy Communion, but it is very profound. Further, it may be a better understanding than some adults in your congregation have of the sacrament.

Include children in the music of worship, such as singing, dancing, and instrumental offerings, just to name a few. Preparation is important. Children need to know where they are to stand, how the music will be held, how the microphone sounds, and so on. It may even be a good idea to reserve a front-row pew for parents or others who can offer a reassuring presence to the child who is leading by providing music in a service. For children who are participating in the music of the congregation, preparation may include teaching or reviewing hymns before worship, practicing words and melodies of certain repeated music (such as the Doxology) at home and in other settings, and using some hymns repeatedly so that they may be learned.

List some ways your church includes children in worship. What new ways can you add? How do these ways affirm and include children?

Participation in the worship services might be enhanced with the use of rhythm instruments during certain psalms or an assignment from the preacher for children to draw a picture of the sermon. One week I asked the children to draw their versions of the seraph after reading the scripture description (Isaiah 6:2). The results were remarkable, and the pictures were posted in the narthex for all to appreciate. Once in a while, I get a few adult participants in these assignments, and I am also thrilled by their creativity! Children's art can be used in so many ways in the bulletin, to illustrate sermons and readings, in devotional publications, and more. With today's technology, many churches are able to scan children's art and publish it immediately on websites or print resources (remember to get parental permission before publishing anything on the web). A criticism I often hear is that children who are drawing or reading during worship are not paying attention to the service itself. This is not true. Many children are quite capable of attending to many different things at once. In fact, they may require it for optimal participation. This is the way they process information.

When we ask people to lead in worship, it's important to be sure children and adults are prepared for their leadership roles before they assume them. Regular training for liturgists, ushers, and acolytes ensures that the leadership experience will be safe and affirming. Our churches should be safe and shame-free places for all people. As we plan worship in our churches, both on Sundays in the sanctuary and in less formal times, we must think each time of how we will include the children and how they can be leaders. Another consideration, one that will take some congregational teaching and learning, is that we should help people understand the difference between worship leadership by children and performance. Our children are not performing for us, an audience, when they lead us in worship. They are leading a congregation.

Education

For most of us, the inclusion of children in our educational ministries is not a new idea. We have been offering classes, both age-grouped and inter-generational, since the beginning of the church. As we create a holistic ministry, we have an opportunity to revisit this and to be intentional about it. The question becomes, in part, "Where might we empower children as leaders in our educational ministries in new ways?" In our educational times, the inclusion of worship education and liturgy will be rewarded by children's increased participation in the worship services. For example, we all probably teach the Lord's Prayer as a routine part of our Sunday morning classes. The children's enthusiastic voices joining the adults in that prayer in worship lends a whole new dimension to it. It would be very powerful for a child to lead that prayer in worship each week. A workshop or series of lessons on the sacraments increases everyone's understanding and comfort level, and it may be done intergenerationally, in family groups, or in age groups. One place for such education might be in new-member groups, if children are a part of those in your church. What would it mean for your church to include children in new-member classes? What would it say to the families?

The question to ask over and over again regarding inclusion of children in educational ministries is "Where are we allowing the children to serve as leaders in this area?" I believe children can be great teachers. Giving them permission to express their opinions in small group discussions and asking for their evaluative input can be quite enlightening. Pairing children and adults in discussion of a video or other such media can give both adult and child new insights.

Children can serve as teachers for younger ones and for adults, and we all know we learn so much when we teach. On Palm Sunday at our church, we transform our classrooms into a very long dining room, with a table on the floor (legs are not unfolded into place) that is long enough to seat about fifty people. Children and adults dress in biblical costume and serve each other food like that eaten in biblical times. One of the classes of older children tells the story of Holy Week, usually through drama, and then we participate in Holy Communion. This year, the children invited the young-adult class to join them. The children taught the adults in an exciting and profound way. The response from the young adults we invited was so enthusiastic that next year we will need a larger space. Please note that in no way does teaching by children negate the presence and practice of adult teachers and supervisors!

These are a few ways one might rethink the educational ministries to further include children as leaders as well as consumers. Inclusion requires careful thought and preparation, so that it will be an experience that will bring the children into closer relationship to God and the community of the church. In my own ministry, at least one of my annual goals relates to this issue, and there is always some new way I am working on including children in educational leadership.

Pastoral Care

Children are natural caregivers. Susan Cox-Johnson ("The Open Arms of Children," *Circuit Rider,* December 1997, page 16) tells of a man in her congregation who had recently lost his beloved wife, who always was at his side as they took communion. On the first communion Sunday after her death, he sat alone in the front pew, with everyone in the congregation seeing his loneliness and feeling his grief. No one could figure out how to help, until an eleven-year-old boy walked up to the front, sat down by the man, and put his arm around him. She reflected that not only did the child spontaneously offer care and comfort, he also acted as a witness to the entire congregation that the Risen Christ was among them.

Children offer such care freely and without condition, and sometimes just their presence is comforting. In September of 1980 my son, David, was three, and I received a call one memorable morning from my sister. I learned that my mother was dying, and I was stunned by grief. I walked David to my neighbor's house in an attempt to take a little time to get myself together, and as I left him with the neighbor, he said, in his little three-year-old voice that will forever echo in my mind, "Don't worry, Mommy, it will be OK." A few days later, David sat on her bed, driving little matchbook cars over her legs and my mother smiled, enjoying every precious moment of his presence.

Children are welcome visitors in many nursing homes and care facilities, and hospitals are appreciating the value of a child's visit in many situations. I was at a nursing home recently and noticed a little boy just sitting with an older man. Neither was saying anything or moving. They just sat together, side by side and leaning on each other, as though resting on each other. Each was caring for the other in a unique and intimate way.

Children also can assist with the church's visitation ministry in many ways: visiting, making cards and gifts, and calling. At one church, families take the altar flowers after worship and the children and adults together deliver them to people limited in their ability to leave home. I've also seen this done with Easter lilies and poinsettias. E-mail is adding a new dimension to caring for each other. Children are included in a prayer chain or in family prayers of intercession for others as another way the children can help care for the church. Even very young children can pray for others as they listen to the prayers of the older children or adults or feel the prayers

How does your congregation provide pastoral care for children? How do children provide pastoral care in your congregation?

of a parent on a lap and in a hug. This is a part of a child's formation as a disciple that is important to recognize and help develop. We need to give children a chance to express their love for the family of God through prayer, visitation, calling, and other forms of caring.

The other side of this is the inclusion of children in the pastoral care given by the staff and congregation. When a child is hospitalized, he or she needs the church to be there to comfort and help heal. When there is a death in a child's family, or when a child's friend dies, there is no more important time to be the church with the child. Being the church means comfort and counseling, offering help in going on with life, as different as it may be. I had a childhood friend whose brother died when she was nine. Sally remembered so much of the death and grieving. She felt abandoned by her parents and the pastor, who didn't say anything except hello to her when he visited them at her home. She missed her brother very much, and clearly understood that he would not be back to play with her again, ever. At the reception after the funeral, she remembered feeling so alone, until Mrs. Green, an older woman from the congregation, took her hand and led her to the table where the mountain of food was laid out. She said, "Sally, I made these cookies just for you." Sally remembered falling into the woman's embrace, and crying until there were no more tears. Mrs. Green was present at Sally's wedding, many years later, and Sally recently read Scripture at her funeral. She was grieving too much to say anything else, but if she could have, she would have told how Mrs. Green held her at her brother's funeral, and made cookies just for her.

Caring for the children of the congregation comes at those times of great pain but also in the celebration of the passages of life.

Inclusion of the children in the life of the church means celebrating losing a baby tooth, earning a driver's license, and moving to a new house. Such love and care gives children glimpses of the kindom of God. It helps children to see that the church of Jesus Christ is at the center of their lives and strengthens them as they grow in faith and move into the world as disciples who will transform the world into the kindom of God.

Evangelism

How can the church include children in the leadership of its evangelism efforts? Again, I think that visibility is key. Children should be included in classes for new members whenever possible, as both participants and leaders. When your church participates in a community event where they may be "advertising" the church through leaflets and invitation, are children included? Some children are very good at this. (Of course, safety issues are important here! Never send the children out without adequate supervision, and supervise all interactions with strangers.) A "Bring a Friend to Sunday School" campaign is another way children can be involved in evangelism efforts. Almost all of the children are interested in inviting their friends to come with them. In fact, I believe many children are better at this than adults.

How are the children of your church included in evangelism and mission efforts? What are new ways they could be included?

When we take our annual all-church-family camping trip in July, we are a large and diverse group and often pique the curiosity of other campers. The children are quick and happy to answer neighboring campers' questions about our identity. "We are our church," they say! The joy and enthusiasm they exhibit demonstrates the value of being a part of a church.

There are a variety of other ways to involve children in evangelism in your church. The primary point is not to underestimate their contributions.

Mission

Mission is another important area in which we must include the children. Service in the community or world allows for faith formation in the expression of one's belief outside of one's self. Children have much energy and enthusiasm for working on projects such as yard clean-up or helping a senior friend clean out a garage or shovel snow. We need to help children see such efforts as an expression of their faith by talking about these actions in the context of the church and the kindom of God. They understand compassion clearly, and are happy to work to help people in need. An annual rummage sale at the church can be interpreted this way to children. Sure, it raises money for the church, but it also benefits many people who come to buy things they may not be able to have otherwise. If the leftovers are donated to a charity, children can help pack up and deliver those items, seeing another missional benefit of the sale. All children can have a place to serve at a rummage sale.

This summer, our church family will go to South Dakota to work at a daycare center. There will be tasks for people of all ages, and children and youth are specifically invited as a part of our group. Some families will use this as their vacation this summer, spending time working on the daycare project and sightseeing on other days. The children and adults will benefit in innumerable ways from these experiences. Their "What I Did Last Summer" essays when they go back to school will be very different from most others!

Including children in discussions where decisions about fundraising, mission, and outreach are discussed helps children understand the purpose of the church in a new way. Participation in these projects is clearly a part of formation as a disciple of Jesus Christ, who transforms the world into the kindom of God. In a holistic children's ministry, our vision is to involve the children in the life of the whole church, not to separate them from the church family or ignore them. Intentional inclusion in worship, education, pastoral care, evangelism, and mission efforts leads to a fuller understanding of faith and the expression of discipleship for all ages.

Chapter 8:
Children on the Playground

Is not this the fast that I choose:
to loose the bonds of injustice,
to undo the thongs of the yoke,
to let the oppressed go free,
and to break every yoke?
Is it not to share your bread with the hungry,
and bring the homeless poor into your house?

Isaiah 58:6-7

There is a little church I know of that sits in the middle of a lovely but faded neighborhood, among houses that were built for one family and now house four or more. The church has held on to some of the old members, the ones who haven't moved to Florida or Arizona or died, and most of them live in the retirement home down the street. There are no children here, at least not in the church. There is a playground, surrounded by a high iron fence. It used to be part of the daycare center at the church, but the daycare center closed more than twelve years ago, and the playground has been sitting, unused, while children stare at it through a fence they cannot scale. "If one of them were to get hurt," the church people say, "we could be sued." There are hundreds of children within blocks of the church, and hundreds of adults who have gifts and talents to share with the church, but the members of the church won't reach out into the community. They don't see it as theirs, and they continue doing what they always have done, the way they've always done it. And their church will die soon, because no one will be left to support it.

The people of the little church don't understand that the kindom of God reaches well beyond what we can see and touch, into the community of people who may be different from "us." That is a paradoxical gift of the kindom, the value of each person no matter what his or her societal or economic status may be. The church of Jesus Christ must present an alternative vision to the exclusionary stance of society and be out among the people as we teach, heal, and share the good news. United Methodist Bishop Kenneth L. Carder (*Interpreter,* May–June 1999, page 19) tells about a visit to an inner-city church where children were very present as greeters, worship leaders, acolytes, and choir members. He commented to one of the church members about their inclusion of the children in the service. The member's response was that they were not "our" children. Another person then reminded the one who had made the comment that since they were Jesus' children they were indeed also "our" children. We must all assume this mission, whether we have our "own" children or not. I don't mean to suggest a division between "ours" and "theirs," because I believe that as Christians all children are our children. We are called to serve, protect, and care for all, as all need the church.

Our mission is to form disciples of Jesus Christ who will transform the world into the kindom of God. A vision is to improve the lives of children and the poor in the community and neighborhood of the church, and there are a great number of ways it can be done. The first step is to understand what the children in your community need, or, in other words, to assess their needs. Laura Dean Ford Friedrich, in *Putting Children and Their Families First: A Planning Handbook for Congregations* (General Board of Global Ministries, 1997), describes five steps for assessing the needs of children in a community and planning a response to those needs. A community assessment is not a difficult task, but it may be time consuming and requires planning a strategy for the use of your time and resources so that you will have useful information at the end. Such planning is a first step, followed by the collection and then interpretation of the information you gather. In the data collection and interpretation steps, there are many existing groups and organizations to assist you, including the Census Bureau, the Children's Defense Fund, local planners, and others. The Children's Defense Fund publishes an annual report on the current state of children in America and maintains statistics on children in each state on its website. One of the most useful listings of information is an annual publication called *Kids Count Data Book,* funded by the Annie E. Casey Foundation. Its mission through the Kids Count project is to describe the most vulnerable children in America through various measures of educational, economic, and social well-being.

In small towns it may be possible to get information through the schools, through government organizations, or even in door-to-door surveys of neighborhoods. But before you launch a door-to-door survey, be sure you're not duplicating the data collection of other groups. After the data is collected and some conclusions and recommendations are made, the information is shared and plans are formed for addressing the needs of the community.

What are new ways your church could reach out to the community to address needs of children and families?

There are a great number of possibilities for ministry with, to, by, and for the children of the neighborhood or community. These include ministries that meet basic needs, such as food, shelter, housing, or health. They also include advocacy ministries in areas such as education, anti-violence, and voter information. They may be new efforts that are one-time events or a series of classes or an ongoing provision of services. Such ministries must include an understanding of the mandate to share a church's resources, including the church building, with the community. You could call this a theology of building use. It needs to be discussed at the administrative council level of your church and defined clearly. Is the church to be used only by the people who are members or is it a form of outreach into the community? How can your church building best be used to serve God in the community? How can the children of your community be ministered to through the use of your building? Obviously building a fence around the playground to exclude children is a statement of the theology of a church, and so is providing space for tutoring, classes in English as a second language, camps, arts, forums on immigration issues and counseling, and so on. Our church, First United Methodist Church of Chicago, offers space to eight different twelve-step programs, some of which have more than one group, creating over a dozen twelve-step meetings in our space each week. It houses meetings of dozens of community groups and advocacy initiatives and is a gathering place for people of many faiths from the city. These people gather at our church to worship together in special services—for example, a service to remember the lives of indigent people who died without known family members and were buried by the county. They gather in our basement to serve the homeless together, and they meet in our church to give Christmas parties for homeless children and their families. We have a theology of building use that says this is a safe and sacred place to address the needs of our community.

Many churches reach into their communities by opening a daycare or preschool in their church building, a response to the need of parents in the community. More parents are entering the work force, more parents are single, and more parents are choosing parenthood later in life when there is an established career to maintain. A preschool or daycare situated in a church offers a solution for these parents. Usually, church-based childcare programs offer a feeling of safety to parents, and often churches will provide some spaces in their programs at reduced costs for those who can't afford full cost. In one church I visited, a wealthy family had established an endowment for need-based scholarships for preschoolers in their church preschool program, and often church members contribute to the church-housed preschool by providing books and toys, by seasonal cleaning and painting efforts, and in one-on-one relationships of members and children, such as tutoring, mentoring, or sharing stories.

First United Methodist of Chicago is in the heart of the business district in the city. There is no community surrounding us, at least not one where children live and play. There are, however, a number of ways we are "in" the community that does exist, reaching out to children and those who care for them. We support neighborhood centers and child-serving agencies in the city with our monetary donations, our work teams, and other kinds of contributions. We educate our congregation about the needs of the children of the city and inform them about pending legislative action that may impact the lives of children. Our staff and lay members serve on the boards of many of the child-serving agencies in the area, and we are active in several grass-roots organizations who are working on systemic changes. We are connecting with the county to work on developing a downtown daycare center near our building, a defined need of the business community surrounding us. We are in touch with several governmental and nonprofit groups that deal with children's issues, such as the Department of Children and Family Services, and are constantly seeking more ways to network with other groups who care about children.

One example of this is our endorsement of the Children's Charter for the State of Illinois. A list of children's basic rights in the areas of family, education, safety, health, economic security, and recreation and the arts, the Charter is a focus point for our church ministries. We endeavor to live out the mandate from the Bishop's Initiative for Children and Poverty to evaluate all we do as a church in terms of how it affects children and the poor. Further, the Charter links us to hundreds of other agencies, faith communities, and organizations who have also endorsed it, and we are beginning to work together to try to live up to the Charter.

When we started Sunday school classes last fall after a summer break, the families of the Sunday school brought school supplies for children in need in the city. The children of the church were able to get into this effort because the items we collected were things these children used and needed, too, and they were items easily found and quite inexpensive. Even our youngest children were able to understand this project. Other churches have given monetary gifts to a local school at the beginning of the year to be used for library books or, in some cases, textbooks. In some communities church members have helped to recycle local businesses' older but still usable computers to a classroom in an inner-city school. Projects like this, where people give their money and goods to assist in the community, should be an ongoing part of every church's ministry.

Another way of addressing the needs of the children in the community is public education. The United Methodist Church has a long history of support of public education. Its Social Principles affirm the importance of public education, and numerous resolutions adopted by the General Conference refer to the church's commitment to supporting public education. There are many ways a local church can become involved. One possibility might be through an adult study class. You could study the church's stance on public education as a beginning point, perhaps with the leadership of a member of a school board or a school administrator. The next session or sessions might then be a study of public education in your community, its history, philosophies, and practices. A visit to the closest public school might be interesting, perhaps led by church members who have attended that school or children who are attending it. A final class session might be a study of recent school board decisions and a discussion of how the church is/might be/should be involved in public education. Presentations by people of the church who serve as volunteers in the schools might also be relevant and informative. As a sending forth, the class might resolve to partner with a school in a variety of ways, become involved in a tutoring effort, or perhaps begin to plan an afterschool or before-school program for the children. An important aspect of this would be contact with the school's administrators, who can help determine where your church might be of most help. For another example, with the cuts in school budgets downsizing or eliminating music and the arts from many schools, the church could offer music and art lessons and mentoring.

One of the most pressing problems in any community today is the prevalence of violence in the community, an issue that faces most of our children in some form every day. Media violence is perhaps the most widespread, but many communities also deal daily with gangs and criminals and domestic violence. This is an area where the church is required to step into the community and raise its voice in many ways. The church can educate people in conflict resolution, in effective parenting, and in communicating in relationships. We can encourage peaceful playthings instead of toy guns

What are your top three priorities related to addressing the needs of children and families in your community? What steps need to be taken to address these priorities?

and other weapons. One church I know had a trade-in day, where children could trade their old violent toys and games for new peacemaking and educational ones. Another church had an "anti-violence" Sunday, and each person made a pledge that day to take some kind of stand against violence. Some were as simple as a single letter to a newspaper editor while other church members made substantial commitments of time, talent, and financial resources to a conflict mediation center. Not every church member can be involved in every issue the church faces, but violence is one that touches everyone in many ways, and response is certain to be enthusiastic. When violence has disrupted your community, a church's response could also include crisis counseling or the loan of its clergy to the families involved for pastoral care.

Reaching into the community provides an opportunity for community groups, churches, and other organizations to form partnerships to address important issues. Local ministerial groups and various steering committees provide a discussion venue for specific issues that may result in a cooperative effort of several groups that is highly effective. Often the people in leadership in such places are very gifted and knowledgeable about the community.

One of the most revealing photographs of the recent past shows a rainbow-colored line of little children interspersed with police personnel and flanked by officers carrying rifles as they escape a gunman at a community center. I know of no one who is able to see that photo without gasping, internally or outwardly, with pain at the violence toward children in our society depicted in that photograph. These children are our children. The church is called to provide solutions to such violence in our communities. The children on the playground are our children, too. Reaching out to them is a way to step out of the basement and serve as disciples who will transform the world into the kindom of God.

Chapter 9
A Voice for the Voiceless

He has told you, O mortal, what is good;
and what does the LORD require of you
but to do justice, and to love kindness,
and to walk humbly with your God?

Micah 6:8

Throughout this book, I have been talking about children's ministry in four ways: ministry to children, with children, by children, and for children. Advocacy is one of the ministries we do that is for children (which is not to say that children are not advocates for other children). It is standing and speaking out for the needs of children and for the inclusion of children as members of the family of God. Needs range from physical needs, such as food and clothing, to emotional needs, such as safe, abuse-free homes and classrooms, to needs that are created by political systems, such as the end of disparities in education for children. Advocacy is the witness the church makes in issues of inclusion and justice on behalf of children in our congregations and all over the world. Obviously, if these are definitions of advocacy, it is no small job. It is a witness that is continuous, never-ending, and often difficult. But advocacy is required as a part of a holistic children's ministry. It is required by our faith, which calls us to respond to the needs of the least of these, those who cannot speak for themselves.

Advocate is a verb, indicating an action. Advocacy can take many forms: mediation, defense, intercession, linking, change, challenge, care, prayer, and many more. Furthermore, all of these actions on behalf of children can be done in a variety of venues, from the local church itself to the federal court system. There are advocacy efforts that teach people about the needs of, current issues related to, and efforts directed to children and their families. Other advocacy efforts are legislative or administrative and help effect change that positively affects children on a local, state, or federal governmental level. There are also advocacy efforts that provide services and support to children and their families, like meals, tutoring, or legal aid, and efforts to increase funding from a variety of sources for children and their families.

In one of the churches I served in, there was a family of three children and a single mom. As they were frequent visitors to the church, we soon became aware not only of unique gifts they offered us but also of particular needs they had. Our first responses were caring and intercession. We helped them with physical needs, and with legal aid when they were evicted from their home. We prayed for the family in our corporate and personal prayers and helped find daycare for the youngest so that the mother could work longer hours. The needs of this family helped us to begin a community clothes closet, where people could trade outgrown children's clothing for larger sizes. This effort grew into a thrift shop carrying clothing and household items sold at moderate prices. Proceeds from the store go to an emergency fund for children. The mother of the family now serves as a volunteer staff member at the thrift shop once a week, and the children are all successfully in school and still in church each week.

This story illustrates advocacy at many levels. Many of the actions of advocacy are apparent in the various ways we, the church, responded to the needs of this family. Each time we spoke up for the needs of this family or against aspects of the system that was making it hard for them to survive, we were advocates. Advocacy is what the church is about.

Throughout the Bible there are stories of people being advocates for children. Jesus was surely a child advocate, and he chastised his disciples for keeping the children from him (Luke 18:15-17). Moses owed his life to women who were advocates for him: his sister, his mother, and the pharaoh's daughter (Exodus 2:1-10). The Syrophoenician woman advocated healing by Jesus for her daughter (Mark 7:24-30). Advocacy is a biblical mandate for Christians.

Advocacy in Our Churches

The United Methodist bishops have called for churches to evaluate all they do in terms of how it affects children. Each time we evaluate our ministry in this light, we act as advocates for children. Speaking up for the rights and needs of children within our churches is essential, because if we don't, they, as the least of these, will be forgotten or assigned to a dark corner of the basement. Speaking up for children in our churches means talking about issues of inclusion and presence. How do we include children in our worship services, in our classes, in our mission trips? One of the most gratifying moments in my recent ministry was at a summer worship service. It was Laity Sunday, and I had nothing to do with the liturgy, organization, or leadership of the services. After five years of ministry there, where I have constantly advocated children's leadership in worship, I was filled with incredible joy when I realized they had included children as leaders that morning, without any suggestion from me. My advocacy efforts were rewarded with this learned response from the laity.

Focus on one advocacy issue for the children or a child in your local church. List ways you can begin to respond as advocates for that child or children.

Other areas of advocacy in your local church include many of the hospitality issues discussed previously. How does your church welcome and include children? Where are children excluded, and why? How does your church recognize the gifts of children and help them use their gifts in service to God? Each of these questions might be a topic of conversation for your administrative council, your staff, or your parents.

In some cases, advocacy means speaking up for the rights of one child in your church. Which of your children has special needs, and how do you address these needs? We put a wheelchair lift into an area of our Sunday school classrooms that is five steps above the rest of the areas. We have no children who need to use that lift right now, but we will be ready when we do. We do have a father of a preschooler who is in a wheelchair, and he can now go to open houses and other activities in his daughter's class.

Being inclusive of children with special needs is rarely a one-time effort, such as the installation of a wheelchair lift. More often, it requires an action plan that evolves over time. Again, it may begin as a recognition of a single need and end in a communitywide effort to change a system. For each identified issue in an individual or family's life, there is probably a corresponding issue in the entire system.

Intergenerational events and ministries are important to helping your advocacy efforts in the local church. Such events provide a place for adults to see and get to know children, to foster understanding among generations, and to lift up special needs of the children. Through these events, you are able to personalize the issues concerning which you are advocating action. A simple example is advocating increased budget allocations for your children's ministry. It is helpful to have an open house in the children's areas, where adults can see that there are not enough supplies, that the toys are shared by too many children, or that the cribs are broken or out of date. One educator I know put signs all over the rooms during an open house, pointing out the lack of certain safety items, the missing puzzle pieces, and so forth.

In intergenerational events, the adults and children get to spend time together, working toward a common goal or learning together. This gives the adults knowledge of the children, who they are and what they need. Events like Advent workshops, vacation Bible school, and others help build bridges across generations, giving an opportunity for advocacy to grow.

Advocacy in the Community

In order to be effective voices for the voiceless in our communities, we must first understand the needs of those communities. Some of the assessment tools mentioned in the last chapter, such as census data and analysis, are again useful here. Additionally, experiencing the community through volunteering in schools, working voter registration drives, or activities with groups who are already in child advocacy helps you understand the needs of the children of the community. Once you have determined some of the needs, then you set priorities for action, based on discussions of your church members. In many communities, it's hard not to rush into every problem you identify, knowing how great the needs are. You will be far more effective, however, if you plan and prioritize and understand as much as you can of the issue before you act.

It is valuable to make connections with other agencies and groups, so that you multiply your efforts through a combined approach. People to connect with include people in the community, such as school officials, police and judicial officers, and other government leaders. There are also church-related groups and centers focused on children. In the Northern Illinois Conference, for example, there are four United Methodist–related child-serving agencies that are always willing to share advocacy information with local churches and work alongside them on specific issues. Other related groups to become acquainted with include the General Board of Global Ministries and the General Board of Discipleship (both general agencies of The United Methodist Church), and conference-level or district-level officers or leaders. The Children's Defense Fund has offices around the country as well as several e-mail lists to which they send information on a regular basis on certain issues. There are many people and groups in the world who want to make a difference for our children. Connections make our efforts stronger and more effective.

Once you, as a church, have an understanding of the needs of children in your community, have set priorities, and have connected with other groups, you may be ready to begin an advocacy action or a ministry directed at advocacy. Some of these are short-term or one-time actions: a march for children's rights, a walk for justice, a stand for children. One-time events like these enthuse and empower people to raise their voices for children. Longer-term actions might include an educational event, such as a seminar on child abuse and neglect, followed by a discussion of current community ministries working against child abuse and a task list for the local church and individuals to use in raising their voices against child abuse. Another longer-term but still simple action would be to assist with local voter registration drives, giving more people opportunities to be heard as they cast their votes.

Advocating changes in legislation and public policy on behalf of children is an area in which you can involve the whole church. Every child advocate should be educating the congregation about the issues. For example, I have been trying to help people in our church understand health insurance issues for children. On church bulletin boards, I have posted the toll-free number for parents to enroll their children. I have written columns in our newsletter on the new health insurance program for families with children and have discussed some of the issues surrounding health insurance, such as infant mortality rates, immunizations, and revised federal poverty guidelines. I included some of the information about the children's health insurance program in e-mail and family mailings. I've helped write and pass legislation at our annual conference encouraging each local church to post the information for their families.

Sometimes, advocating changes in legislation includes advocacy for changes in budgets. Children are often neglected when budgets are devised, at every level of government and often of our churches. The costs of not spending on children and child-related programs and ministries are greater for us in the long term. An example of this is the Head Start program. Head Start has many advantages, but one is in long-term savings of tax money. Their early education gives the children the skills and knowledge they need so that they can start school prepared to learn. The public schools are then able to focus on the teaching appropriate to the grade level for all children who enter. Remedial education costs more than programs like Head Start. Every state has agencies or organizations which are working on budget advocacy. For example, at this time, the tobacco company lawsuit settlement has resulted in large amounts of unexpected money being allocated to many states. Concerned groups in Illinois have formed a coalition to advocate that a fair share of the tobacco money be used for children's needs, particularly child health concerns. Churches who are advocates for children can speak up and be heard on issues such as this by joining such coalitions.

Brainstorm three or four ways your church can immediately become more involved in child advocacy. Devise a timetable to accomplish it.

Advocacy for children can come through focus on particular issues, such as child abuse. I am currently developing such a focus for our church. It will begin with a short-term study, three meetings of a small group of adults with an interest in this topic. At the first meeting, we will discuss the issue in current literature and take a look at The United Methodist Church's stance on the issue. In the second meeting, we will look at current statistics in the United States, Illinois, and the Chicago area and invite a guest speaker to provide additional perspective. The third meeting will include a strategizing of actions we can take to help prevent child abuse. One of these actions will be to review our own church's policy on child-abuse prevention. Whether we will approach the issue from a federal, state, or local focus, or some combination of the three, will be up to the group. Perhaps we will begin with a churchwide educational effort, utilizing other classes, the pulpit, and the written word to educate. Or maybe we will take it to a district or conference level and enlist other churches to work with us. As a child advocate, I will have raised the issue in ways that empower our church members and friends, making them child advocates in this area of child abuse. They then become voices for the voiceless who will extend the effort into the world.

Another way a church can educate people about issues is by hosting or sending representatives to attend community topical forums, such as a candidate forum where all candidates for a certain office are invited to come and discuss their views on issues affecting children. (Be careful to invite all candidates to such a forum, so that the church is not accused of supporting one particular candidate, or your tax status could be questioned!) Short-term efforts in political advocacy include, again, voter registration drives, poll transportation, writing letters to candidates and to elected officials about specific issues, and visiting elected officials. Urging support of legislative issues and policies that affect the well-being of children is an important part of a child advocate's job.

Your continued education as a child advocate enables you to be more effective in speaking out about issues affecting children. There are many opportunities in the church for learning. Among them are district and conference events for training and support of advocates and events sponsored by professional organizations for Christian educators.

Advocacy for children is a very important part of a holistic children's ministry in our churches. It combines elements of seeking justice, kindness, and piety to fulfill the biblical mandate to serve the least of these. Advocacy, standing for children and giving voice to our values and beliefs for improving the lives of children in our midst, our community, and our world, is an integral part of God's call to children's ministry. Whether it is the act of empowering parents to care for their children or assisting in writing letters of protest about an issue affecting children's rights, advocacy is speaking up for our children as a response to our call. Advocacy can change the lives of our children, letting them feel and recognize God's great love for them through the words we speak on their behalf. Efforts by a church in the arena of child advocacy are giant steps out of the basement.

Chapter 10:
These Are Our Children, Too

And he said to them, "Go into all the world and proclaim the good news to the whole creation."

Mark 16:15

The world has become a better place for children in the past several decades. UNICEF, in its *State of the World's Children 2000* report, tells us that the mortality rates for children under five have decreased dramatically, primarily due to the near elimination of polio and the vaccines for neonatal tetanus and measles. Blindness from vitamin A deficiency has been greatly reduced, and substantial progress has been made toward the eradication of mental retardation from iodine deficiency. Great advances have occurred for children, especially in the area of health.

But still, however, there are millions of children all over the world who need help urgently, who face a variety of harmful life conditions every moment of every day. UNICEF reports that more than 30,000 children under five years old die every day of preventable causes. There are more than 12 million HIV/AIDS orphans. More than 600 million children live in absolute poverty. Estimates suggest that 250 million children in developing countries are working. These are just a few of the tragic statistics about the children of the world.

Compassion for the least of these calls us to reach out beyond our own country. A holistic vision of children's ministries requires reaching beyond

How is your church involved in global concerns of children?

the walls of our churches and the borders of our own country to the rest of the world.

I remember the church of my childhood tried to be informed about the needs of the world. It wasn't easy, as we relied on secondhand and often dated information. We made real efforts to improve the lives of children in other countries, often through monetary offerings. The words "for the starving children of . . ." ring in my memory. A holistic approach to children's ministry requires a global approach in addition to our church-based and community-based ministries, especially in this age when we can interact with people all over the world in a variety of ways with very little cost or effort. Information about the lives of people of the world is at our fingertips twenty-four hours a day. Mission trips for education or service are readily available to anyone who can raise the time and money to go. Pictures and videos of every kind of international problem, from starving children to the working conditions of children, are available in an instant. We cannot claim ignorance as an excuse for avoiding this global mandate.

One way to approach the wide topic of world concerns of children is to focus on particular issues. A good beginning point might be the United Nations Convention on the Rights of the Child. It is an agreement that, at this writing, has been signed and ratified by every U.N. member state in the world except two: Somalia and the United States. Somalia has no government to ratify a treaty at this time, but there is no such difficulty hindering the United States. Our attempts at ratifying it have been stalled in a political logjam that will only be broken when our congresspersons hear voices of millions of us asking for ratification. The treaty articulates human rights for children, including the right to education; protection against discrimination on the basis of race, gender, or religion; the right to health care; protection against abuse, neglect, or injury; the right to a name and nationality; protection from exploitation for economic gain; protection against torture; and the right to freedom of thought and expression. It is a statement of the very basic rights a human being should have in any country. Efforts by a church might include educating the congregation or community about the treaty and writing letters to the President and Congress urging ratification.

Another issue that might be a rallying point for a church is child prostitution. I remember my shock when I was in seminary at learning that child prostitution existed in "other countries." I guess it wasn't a topic that would have intersected my life at other points, and it just hadn't occurred to me that such evil existed anywhere. The travesty of international "trafficking," as the business of international child prostitution is called, is reflected even in the fact that UNICEF classifies these children as being "in especially difficult circumstances." The reality of child prostitution is that one of the destinations for the children who are duped or forced into the trade is the United States. Estimates in 1996 held that more than one hundred thousand children were in prostitution in the U.S. and Canada. Around the world, more than two million children each year are compelled to begin practicing prostitution, half of these in Asia. Trafficking makes more money for organized crime than anything except drugs and guns, and this profit source is growing (*Working Together,* the quarterly news journal of the Center for the Prevention of Sexual and Domestic Violence, Summer 2000, pages 1 and 2). Child prostitution is clearly an international and growing issue, one that churches can take a stand against. Here they can begin to make a global difference for children.

Throughout The United Methodist Church, there are many groups working to make a global difference. One current issue is the continuing presence of land mines. According to Save the Children, land mines kill between eight thousand and ten thousand children every year. There is one land mine for every twelve children in the world. The countries most affected by mines include Afghanistan, Angola, Cambodia, Mozambique, Iraq, Bosnia-Herzegovina, Croatia, and Somalia. They were laid down in wars primarily beginning with the Second World War, and if not exploded or removed, they remain active and lethal for decades. In addition to the immediate danger of the mines, they obstruct roads for supplies and people and create danger zones out of land that had previously been producing food. Work on this issue is both educational and political. Some annual conferences have passed resolutions calling for a ban on land mines and urging the President to sign the treaty banning land mines. Many are ensuring the continuing education of church members on this issue, through brochure availability and special programs in the church.

The list of issues a church might become involved in regarding the needs of children around the world is endless. Unless you select specific issues for study and response, and set priorities, you could find yourself overwhelmed with information and needs. I have experienced jumping from one issue to another without an adequate response from the congregation or a sense of accomplishment or completion on any project, and it isn't a healthy place to be! This is also an area where you will find yourself working with other ministry groups or committees in the church, in addition to the children's council or the commission on education. Combining the efforts of your mission and social justice groups with your focus on making a global difference for children is helpful in terms of both time and effort.

Research ways your conference and the general church is working on global projects specifically affecting children. How is your church already involved?

A congregation can become involved in issues in several ways. The first is nearly always education. What is the issue? What can we learn about it? What do people already know about it, how does it affect them, and what is a Christian response? Are there several possible responses? How are these issues of faith? Hosting forums that address these and related questions is one way to educate, as is a lecture or video presentation by an authority on the issue, supplemented by brochures and other handouts. Again, the children of your church can be included in these educational efforts. Once again, a holistic approach to children's ministry recognizes the need for inclusion of all age groups in our ministries.

Following the educational efforts is a response by the congregation. What do they want to do with the information shared and learned? Responses might include a monetary gift or gifts of goods needed in specific areas. A response might be an ongoing effort to make a change in a political system, such as a resolution at an annual conference, letters to an editor, or a series of work projects at a mission site. One of the responses of the congregation might be prayer for the children affected by the issue they have been studying. Perhaps an ongoing prayer effort would be a way your church would respond. Even one prayer dedicated to an issue is a response to the issue.

Once we planned a large educational effort on the needs of the children of Haiti, which extended throughout the Sunday morning activities for much of the fall, with a final program near Thanksgiving. We offered time in classes and mission moments in worship centered on education of the congregation, and there was a weekday study and several additional programs with a focus on Haiti. Topics for learning included poverty, culture and customs, slavery and child labor, and health. Evie was a child in the second grade classroom who attended church and Sunday classes as a visitor with a neighboring family. Her own parents worked on Sunday and hadn't yet become involved in the church. Evie was one of those children who never quite seemed to be paying attention. She was constantly distracted by the toys and books in the room and appeared to be uninterested in the whole Haiti focus. I was absolutely shocked to receive a note just before Christmas, with a generous check for the Haiti project. Her mother wrote that Evie had spent many dinner hours over the past several months talking about the children of Haiti, and she had taught the entire family about the conditions under which Haitian children live. Evie inspired the family to look together at some additional resources at the library and discuss what response they might make as a family. They decided to give some of the money that would have been spent for Christmas gifts to our Haiti projects, the check in the envelope. Evie's mother thanked me for helping Evie see the world beyond herself in such a way that she could share it with others important to her, and for making it possible for the entire family to participate in this unique way in our Haiti focus. The note from Evie's mother was encouraging to me personally but also verified the importance of including children in global efforts.

It isn't necessary to reinvent the wheel when undertaking these efforts in relating to children around the world. There are existing curricula and other resources that can make your efforts more comprehensive and much easier. For example, the Children's Fund for Christian Mission annually supports specific projects, some in the United States and some abroad, that benefit children. A primary criterion for selecting the projects is the ease with which children might understand themselves as being in mission. A packet is published each year with educational activities relating to specific projects around the world, along with a map and suggestions for further study. The activities suggested are written in such a way that the children will think about cultural differences and similarities, discover the issues facing people around the world, and respond with monetary gifts and a greater understanding of discipleship in the world.

Hope for the Children of Africa is an appeal from the Council of Bishops of The United Methodist Church to address some of the needs of the children of Africa to bring relief as well as restoration to the people. It is a part of the Bishop's Initiative on Children and Poverty and is a churchwide mission effort. Many areas of the church are currently working on or have recently published resources to assist in the interpretation of the appeal. Resources are available to help you educate both children and adults in your church about the appeal and to aid you with projects as a response to the learning.

It is very important to be certain the projects you choose are legitimate. It is a sad but true fact that there are many groups which purport to serve children around the world but which use most of the donations they receive to serve the people who run them. These groups are very experienced in getting contributions, so it's important to check out all groups and projects with your denomination's boards or agencies before supporting them. One of the advantages of giving monetary donations through the Advance Specials of The United Methodist Church is that one hundred percent of the money goes to the project. Administrative costs are covered by the church through other sources.

Another way to help your church's children relate to children around the world is to establish relationships with churches in other countries. One way to do this is through missionaries, either by inviting them to share with the children or corresponding with them. Some churches have set up a pen-pal list, with children corresponding with other children around the world either by e-mail or by letters. One church in the Northern Illinois Conference has established a relationship with a church in Angola, a kind of sister-church relationship. The two churches have worshiped together via satellite videoconferencing equipment, they have prayed for each other, and they share notes about their activities. The relationship is two-way; both churches benefit from their "sisterhood," and both churches understand each other in new ways.

Issues will continue to arise that affect the well-being of the children of the world. Reaching out and relating to children around the world requires an intentional approach, whether it is issue-based or project-specific or a combination of the two. Jesus called us to proclaim the good news to all the world. Such proclamation is done through serving where there is need and understanding the differences that make us all unique. The good news is proclaimed in the ways we reach beyond ourselves in sharing the kindom of God.

*If the whole body were an eye, where would the hearing
be? If the whole body were hearing, where would the
sense of smell be? But as it is, God arranged the members
in the body, each one of them, as he chose.*

1 Corinthians 12:17-18

In "A Church for All God's Children" the final area or subsystem included
in a holistic ministry with, by, for, and to children is a system of administrative supports for this ministry. In any system, such supports are the
skeleton of the body, the frame that coordinates efforts, holds the larger
system together, and enables united efforts on behalf of many subsystems.
These supports are the glue that sticks all of our ministries together. Administrative supports are the various groups and individuals who accomplish
much of the planning and administering of ministries regarding children.
Such supports are also the place for much of the evaluation of ministry. As
such, they ensure the continuation of efforts that benefit children of the
church and world.

A subsystem of administrative supports fits within the general ministry
of the church at many levels. For example, many churches have a children's
council or a children's advisory council that has the primary evaluative
function for ministries affecting children. It works in tandem with a larger
church council, perhaps called the council of ministries or the administrative council, to coordinate efforts and allocate church resources. Since we
minister with children, ideally a children's council should be made up of
adults and children. It should have some kind of access to the pastoral staff,

How are the subsystems in your church aligned to support one another ? How do they compete with one another?

perhaps through a staff enabler or by meeting on a regular basis with the staff and pastor(s). Here is a place children's ministries can easily be relegated to the "basement" when the council is not given staff access or another place where their work can be shared with other governing bodies of the church.

On the other hand, your children's ministries can also be overadministered, as I witnessed in one fairly large church a number of years ago. On the surface, it appeared that there was a wonderful subsystem of administrative support for children's ministries. There were several volunteer superintendents of age levels and a paid Christian educator whose responsibilities included only children's ministries. There was also a terrific music department, with its own chairperson for each age level and several musical groups for children as well as adults. Further, there was a missions work area, which also had chairpersons of various age groups and even a coordinator of intergenerational mission work. Finally, there was also the nursery school, a five-day program with totally different music and education people. It seemed like everyone I met at this church had some area of which he or she was in charge. I realize this sounds like a megachurch with thousands of members, but it wasn't. A fairly typical suburban church, it had about 750 members.

One Christmas, the preschool choir was involved in one of those large productions somewhat related to the Christmas story. Their part was not large, but the director felt it was quite important. Unbeknownst to her, the mission group had also planned an informal sorting and wrapping of Christmas gifts for needy families that afternoon at the local thrift shop, which involved many of the preschoolers' families. Further complicating the afternoon, the nursery school had planned a cookie party. All of these were important events, at least to my preschoolers, and we had a tough time sorting out the day so that we could attend more than one. By the time we reached the church for the big Nativity pageant, my kids were exhausted and didn't care whether or not they were in it. Less than two-thirds of the choir even showed up, and several of the ones who did appear sat down in the middle of their song. One little guy even lay down on the floor of the stage! (Not my child, I swear.)

There are all kinds of lessons to be learned from this story, but the main point is this: Had there been some sort of a council or coordinator with knowledge of all that the preschoolers were to participate in that day, some changes could have been made to make it easier on the children and families, encouraging full participation in all of the events. Some might suggest that this is the job of the paid Christian educator in the church. Perhaps at times it is. But a children's council or an administrative council could have made efforts to tie all of these events together so that they all had more meaning than each had individually. If it couldn't coordinate the efforts of so many groups, perhaps it would have changed the schedule or at least realized that there were a few too many leaders for the number of children and families we had. In this instance, if the administrators were to be the glue that held everything together, our Sunday looked like one of the art projects of one of my favorite three-year-olds: saturated with glue to the point where it all slides apart.

One of the biggest difficulties I had in the "Church of the Preschool Divisions" mentioned above is that we didn't seem to have a good understanding of why we were doing the ministries we were doing. While we were bound together by common life stage and interest, there was no one bringing the issues into focus for us or encouraging us to relate our ministries to a greater understanding of our faith. There was no group of persons articulating a mission of the church and helping us relate our work to that mission. If the mission of the church is to make disciples of Jesus Christ who will transform the world into the.kindom of God, how did the programs planned on that busy Sunday relate to or encourage that mission?

Another function of administrative supports for children's ministries is just what the name implies: support. What person or group in the church stands up for children's ministries when budget time rolls around? How does the church understand children as a part of the annual stewardship campaign, and who ensures that there continues to be inclusion of children in the life of the church? These are just a few examples, but when left to just one person, much of this may not be done. Furthermore, it is much more effective when many are advocating for children's ministries. This is especially true in the area of budgeting, when children's ministries have been so often given a low and meager amount. This is another way to relegate children's ministries to the metaphorical basement. Without enough funds, it is very difficult to begin to create a safe and inviting ministry.

Support means to advocate fulfilling the needs of children's ministries, but it also includes an evaluative function. Without evaluation of our ministries, we can never be sure we are meeting the needs of the church or serving the people in the ways they need to be served.

Support also means to ensure that there are enough trained teachers, mentors, helpers, and caregivers involved in children's ministries. It means providing enough and appropriate supplies and equipment, prioritizing the use of space, and securing space in the newsletter, the web page, and other

What are the functions of the individuals or groups who provide administrative support for children's ministry in your church?

places for publicity and announcements. Administrative support is multifaceted and will vary from one church to another.

In addition to supporting children's ministries, an administrative structure or subsystem ensures the continuity of ministry from one month or year to the next and from one set of staff members to the next. Continuity helps create a security among the church members, a knowledge that the ministries they expect for their children and families will be available to them. Continuity also helps the church create and remember its history and tradition. Here, administrative supports become a sort of depository for stories and events repeated over time. In my current church, our children's council helps provide support for our annual retelling of the story of the Nativity at Christmas time. The council members help out in a variety of ways, including costumes. Our littlest children are always sheep in the story, and we have many dated but still usable sheep costumes. Each year, as we plan for the event, the stories of past sheep adventures are repeated and remembered. Last year, as we were planning, one mom on the council sadly lamented that this was their family's last time to have a sheep in the story. The children's council has supported a tradition important to the people of the church.

I have mentioned the children's council several times in this chapter, but it is only one of several possible administrative bodies or individuals that support children's ministry in a church. A council works well for us, in our church, because it is made up of a wide variety of people who are concerned about children's ministry—teachers, parents, other members. I admit that there are no children on the current children's council, as we haven't figured out a way to deal with a transportation issue related to the inclusion of children in council meetings. We include children as decision makers in other ways, and I am sure we will have children and youth as members of the council in the near future. It seems to us to be an important issue.

Our children's council is about a dozen individuals with interests in children's ministry. As I said above, they are teachers, parents, concerned members, male and female. They meet about every other month, and often have conversations via the Internet as a way to address immediate concerns. They sponsor events with their presence and talents, help ensure the presence of children in worship and their participation in other aspects of church life, and help determine topics for advocacy efforts. The council decides on special offerings and mission events for and from the children and has the oversight of budget items relating to children. Another important way this children's council serves is in evaluating my work in relation to them. They help me formulate priorities for my ministry and let me know how they perceive my role as a minister with children. They also sometimes keep me balanced when I overenthusiastically propose a new ministry initiative or suggest a creative new approach that might be just a bit impractical in this setting.

In my previous church, there was a commission on education with the functions of my current children's council, and in some churches I know, there is an education ministry group with children's ministry responsibilities. One concern I have about equating children's ministries and education commissions or ministry groups is that often this also equates children's ministries with Sunday school, to the exclusion of other areas important to a holistic ministry with, by, for, and to children of the church. Helping children to grow as disciples who will transform the world into the kindom of God is our mission, and education is a part of that, but only a part. Even if you have no experience at all with the church and children in the church, if you have read this far into this book you realize that helping children grow as disciples reaches well beyond education. If children's ministries are entirely the responsibility of your education group, I urge you to meet with the church council and staff and find new ways each ministry group or committee can work to ensure a holistic ministry for children. One way to compose a children's advisory council might be to appoint representatives from each committee or ministry group in the church to a council concerned with children's issues and needs and inclusion of children into the life of the church. This would provide a wide representation of people from the whole church.

Once a children's advisory council is established, it is very important to help the council clarify their mission and understand their roles in the church community. I was a new member of a church where a fall festival was a big event. Each year, the children's ministry group planned for months to create a bigger and better, and more lucrative, event than the year before. Individuals worked for months on county-fairlike crafts and displays, and food was cooked and frozen months ahead of time to feed the anticipated crowds of people. Great efforts were taken to ensure safe and fun games for children, and a first aid center was one of the first to be plotted on the site map. People talked for weeks ahead of time about what they were donating to the pie auction or who was staffing the dunk tank. Pleas for volunteer workers were the first announcements each week in worship for two months before the event, and written requests filled every bulletin and newsletter. The big day of the festival came, and it seemed quite successful.

Lots of money was raised, and people had a wonderful time eating, playing, and buying. I couldn't help wondering, though, why this was a church event. It did serve to build the community of the church—something important but not necessarily a primary task of the children's ministry council. But what made it different from any other fall festival in the area? What was the purpose of this event for the children? With some deep digging, I finally learned that twelve years ago, the event had been started with the mission of fundraising for a child of the church who had mounting medical bills from an automobile accident. It had been repeated the following year because it was fun. The proceeds benefited the general church budget, but over the years they sometimes were able to put aside sums for needed equipment or supplies for children. While not an unworthy event, it seemed to me that we had put out a lot of time and energy for a project where fun was the mission. In the long run, there was a mission behind the festival, but it needed to be revisited each year rather than simply repeated. Clarity of mission is important not just for the overall program but for each event, study, and mission project. Articulating a mission enables an understanding of each part of our children's ministries as ministry, not only related to the church but also important to the church.

In addition to a children's council or some similar structure, other church staff need to be part of the administrative supports for children. Pastors, Christian educators, music directors, church administrators and clerical staff, and custodial staff all need to be viewed as advocates and supports of systems of children's ministries. Each staff member has specific gifts to offer your council, and the council can provide them with valuable feedback and help in their ministries. There is a custodian in a church near me who sees his work as a ministry of hospitality and love. He not only ensures a safe and clean environment but also greets the church community and works with them on many building-related projects. He sees his involvement in children's ministry as an important part of his job and works closely with the chair of the children's council and supports them in many ways.

Communication is always an issue on church staffs, and the involvement of staff in children's ministries requires a clear understanding of limits and expectations. Communication can be facilitated by the establishment of lines of communication. Using a very simple example, if the custodian needs to be included in a discussion, not all of the people on the council will call the custodian, but only one will! Or, for another example, critical issues will be taken from the council to a staff meeting by staff members rather than publicly aired in general conversation around the church. However it works in your church, defining channels of communication facilitates support from staff.

An ongoing need for a holistic children's ministry is to train and provide resources to people relating to it. Staff, in order to be the administrative supports they can be, may need special training in child safety, CPR and first aid, or perhaps basic pastoral care or listening skills. Teachers and children's workers need to develop specific skills. One example is simple first aid for a cut. All teachers need to know that to care for a bleeding cut on a person, they must follow several steps: put on gloves, cleanse the cut, and apply the bandage. Similarly, when the fire alarm sounds, there are exact steps to take, and when a child hurts another in the classroom, there are procedures to be followed. Training teachers and other children's workers involves teaching them basic organizational patterns and routines and the use of equipment and supplies. It includes understanding the components of a curriculum resource and of supplemental materials. Training includes the review of the church's child-abuse protection policy as well as of the discipline policy. Every teacher-training workshop or meeting, every children's workers' meeting, will have its own agenda and elements for inclusion.

Appendix A of this book (pages 97-99) contains a sample of a workshop for initial training of Sunday class teachers as an example of a format that could be used. It is not inclusive of everything that any situation might call for, but is a basic format that you may adapt for use in your church setting.

A holistic approach to ministry with, by, for, and to children requires consultation with and consideration of other parts of the church. A system of children's ministries is only a subsystem of the ministries of the church, and a change in one system affects the rest in ways you cannot predict unless you consult with the others. I might have decided that children's ministries is the most important system in the church, but consideration of the other systems makes our ministries much more successful and easier. Furthermore, being part of a system implies that other parts are working with you toward a common mission. A common mission, helping to form disciples who will transform the world into the kindom of God, requires assisting each other as we move toward that goal.

As the church moves toward its goal, one of the areas needing attention from administrative supports more and more commonly is issues relating to crosscultural and multicultural concerns. The generation of children born between 1982 and 1999 is the most diverse in their racial and ethnic backgrounds of any in the history of the United States. Nearly 8% of these children would identify themselves as multiethnic. Only 63% of them are non-Hispanic white (statistics from *Now Is the Time!* video and discussion guide published by Discipleship Resources, 1999). Places like the children's advisory council can be one setting where we can teach and learn about each other. We can say we are inclusive and welcome people of all races and

Essential Resource:
Now Is the Time!
video
(see page 109)

ethnic backgrounds, but unless we have safe spaces where we can share our traditions and expectations together, we are not. Respecting, honoring, sharing, and caring about our differences brings us closer together as God's family.

Finally, I need to say another word about evaluation. One of the primary purposes of such supports is to help evaluate ministries, both formally and informally, so that changes (improvements) can be made that benefit the church. Formal evaluation might be in the form of intentional surveys, questionnaires, or polls of church members. Informal methods of evaluation include conversations in meetings or individual discussions. Evaluation is not always an easy task, as when favorite ministries are not being supported or groups need to be changed. Evaluation suggests changes will be made based on some group consensus, and this is not always a popular activity in a church. When changes are made and the church moves forward in new directions, there will always be a group who wants to go back to the way things used to be. In your ministry, you have probably come up against this "back to Egypt" committee several times. These are the people who, in the course of evaluation, always want to go back to the way things were in another time, just like the Hebrews who wandered for forty years in the desert with Moses wanted to go home. We are continually being called into the future, and it is helpful to reroute the "back to Egypt" committee by involving them in the evaluative process, while still listening to their stories of Egypt.

Chapter 12
Caring for the Children

Jesus said, "Let the little children come to me, and do not stop them; for it is to such as these that the kingdom of heaven belongs." And he laid his hands on them and went on his way.

Matthew 19:14-15

Caring for children in a pastoral way is not one of the nine identified areas of "A Church for All God's Children." I believe that is because it is an implicit part of all nine of the areas described. Nothing in children's ministry can be accomplished without this caring, because it creates an environment of trust and hope that facilitates other kinds of ministry. Furthermore, it is not limited to a certain type of child. Rather, all children experience times when they are in need of care. This kind of care might involve physical needs, but more often it relates to emotional and spiritual growth or distress. The following story shows many facets of caring for the children.

Martin was a little boy, about six years old. His family had been active in my church since before I joined. They were in leadership roles, active and attending most events, and also busy with jobs in the world beyond the church. Dad was an attorney, and Mom was a public relations executive for a large downtown firm. Martin had a sister, three years younger than he was, named Sara, and a caregiver who stayed with the children every weekday, named Harriet. Sara and Martin attended Sunday classes each week, and were energetic and enthused about participating. Shortly after Christmas one year, at our quarterly teachers' meeting, the preschool teacher mentioned that she was concerned about Sara, in that she seemed withdrawn and uninterested in class, a change from past behavior. Martin's teacher added that he, too, had not been himself lately, and after a bit of conversation, we agreed that they were probably coming down with a winter "bug," or perhaps were just worn out from all their activities. Two weeks later, the preschool teacher came to me indicating that Sara had new visible bruises on her face, and last week she had worn a band-aid over her eye. This family had no history of abusive behavior, and Martin had no new bruises or unexplained injuries, so we decided that I would follow up with a phone call to check on Sara. Mom gave me very reasonable explanations for Sara's injuries but seemed distant as she talked to me. I assured Mom that we were here for her and the family, and let her know a second time that we cared about them. I heard a click on the line, as though someone was listening in, but no one else spoke. The next Sunday, Martin sought me out, and we went to the "parlor" to talk, a busy place, but we sat out of the way where we could talk together. Martin needed my help, he said. He had heard me say on the phone that I cared for them, so he wanted me to know that he was afraid his dad was moving out. His mom and dad were fighting a lot, he said, and he had heard the words *divorce* and *lawyer,* and he just wondered if I could stop it. I asked him if either of them had hurt Sara or him at any time, during the fights or any other time, and Martin said no. He told me how Sara had hurt her eye and face in two separate accidents, one while Mom was there and one under Harriet's care. This was consistent with what Mom had said. Being assured the children were physically safe, I moved into the divorce issue. I asked Martin if he would like me to talk to his mom and dad to see if they wanted help, and explained that I knew some people whom it would be good for Mom and Dad to see to work on their differences. I tried to help him understand that while I could listen to his parents, there were people who were much better at it than I was. He agreed to let me talk to his parents, so I asked if he wanted to be with me when I did. He did not want to be there, but said it was OK if I told them how worried he was. We talked for a little while longer about divorce. He told me about some of his friends whose parents were divorced, and I mentioned that all marriages are sometimes difficult, and that working on issues doesn't necessarily mean divorce. I also said that if a divorce did occur, it didn't mean that either of his parents loved him any less, and that I was sure they would do all they could to make sure he knew that. I told him I would pray for his family, asking God to be with them all and help them through this difficult time, and then asked if we could pray together. I'll never forget his words of gratitude, or the tear that rolled down his little cheek as we prayed together.

Martin's story is a true story from my ministry, although his name was not really Martin, nor were some of the other details exact, as I wanted to protect his identity. For those of you who absolutely need to know what happened, I add that his parents did get into a church-related counseling center, and Martin and I had several more talks together over the years. His parents divorced when Martin was nine, and Martin and Sara became like a third of their generation in experiencing the divorce of their parents (*Now Is the Time!* video and discussion guide; General Board of Discipleship, 1999). Sara and Martin are doing well, living with their mother, and still attending that church.

Care for children was a part of Jesus' ministry. He healed children, Jairus' daughter, for example (Mark 5:21-43), and took time out of his busy ministry to talk with them and bless them. In Matthew, he asked that the children be brought to him and he "laid his hands on them and went on his way" (Matthew 19:15). That he laid his hands on them is particularly interesting.

The Interpreter's Dictionary of the Bible explains that the laying on of hands imparts a blessing but that it also indicates the giving of a sort of physical and spiritual health and wholeness to the person being touched (Abingdon Press, 1962; Volume 2, page 521). Jesus cared for the children in a unique way, calling us to do the same, blessing the children and helping them to physical and spiritual health.

The time and place for caring for our children is whenever we have contact with them and their families. In all cases, we who profess to care about children must be ready to care for them. Being ready to offer this care means that we need to be available and approachable to children. We need to be where they can see us and talk with us. Last week, I was greeting people after worship, and four-year-old Abby greeted me with her normal hug, but instead of her usual response to my "How are you?" query, she said, "Cocoa died." She didn't seem particularly upset, but wanted me to know, probably just because she saw me and I was available.

When Martin found me, in the previous story, I was in a busy hallway, and we went to the parlor to talk. My office in that church was in a secluded part of the building (the metaphorical basement, again!) and taking him there to talk would not have been a good idea. We would have been away from the activity of the day, and my child safety training reminds me not to be totally alone with any child. In the parlor, we could talk privately and yet be seen by many people. The parlor was also safe for Martin because it was a familiar place to him, whereas my office was not. Martin had heard me talking on the phone with his mother, but he also found me in the church because I was available. Being available for children to express their concerns, or for families who are needing some extra help, is easier now with e-mail. Most of the children of my Sunday school have an e-mail address, and they know mine.

Availability is not the same as being present for the children. Presence, especially a listening presence, is a basic element of caring for children. Children know when a person genuinely cares about them and when there is superficiality or pretense. They also know when we are hurried and not really listening. Through Martin's experience of me in the Sunday classes and through what he heard me say on the phone, Martin trusted me to listen to him, to hear some very deep concerns. A six-year-old, Martin probably thought I had more power to intervene in the situation than I did, and I was careful to explain to him what I thought I could do to help. Presence with a child means attending and responding to the child's needs through appreciation, listening, and affirmation. Sometimes, it means helping the child to understand you are not available at a specific time but will be with him or her at another time. For many children a ministry of presence will be demonstrated not just by the pastor or minister of education but by a teacher in a classroom, a nursery caregiver, or a storyteller. Note that in Martin's story, it was not the church professional who first suspected that Martin and Sara needed some help, it was their teachers.

Sometimes, all a child needs is to be heard. At other times, you need to engage in some sort of advocacy for the child. Before I could fully enter into listening to Martin, I needed to be sure he and Sara were physically safe. Twice in my years of ministry I have had to report suspected incidents of child abuse. In one case, the parent was very upset, and "reported" me to the senior pastor, who would have been in a very awkward place if we had not had a child-abuse prevention policy in place in the church, which required the specific actions I took. Advocacy might also be required for children who express physical needs (hunger, clothing, shelter) or who need someone to speak up for them. For example, there was a child in one of my churches who really was bored in her classroom because she was so bright. Our Sunday school teacher noticed it at church and mentioned it to me. I talked to the child and parents and helped them work through the public school system so she could be tested for the gifted program at the school. Advocacy for a child in the context of caring for the child takes many different forms.

Spirituality is what makes us different from a public school counselor or a social worker. We can offer the additional help that faith brings to life situations. Note that in the story of Martin I told him I would pray for him, and then prayed with him. Other ways I could have brought in our faith tradition might have been to help him remember a Bible story which was similar to his own situation or to talk with him about a theological issue that related to his experience. Obviously, with a six-year-old, I wouldn't have used the term *reconciliation,* but it was implied in my words. Martin knew that the church is a place where we pray, talk about God, and find ways that God is working in our lives and stories. I believe he sought me out for this discussion in part because he expected a faith response from me and believed it would be helpful to him. Religious content is important in responding to the care needs of children.

There are many ethical and legal issues surrounding care of children in this counseling, advising, mentoring way. One of the tasks of a children's council might be to investigate the laws about these issues for your city and state, because they differ from place to place. For example, whether or not teachers in the church are mandated reporters of suspected child abuse is an issue that varies geographically. Other legal issues you might want to be aware of relate to custody issues, such as whether or not a noncustodial parent can grant permission for a child to go out of the church. Finally, it's important to be sure you, other staff members, and volunteers at your church are protected by liability insurance relating to counseling and practice of ministry with children.

One of the primary ethical issues, however, is generic, common to all places. That issue is confidentiality. A child's trust requires that you handle his or her situation in a confidential way. I asked Martin if it was OK to talk to his parents and if he wanted to be with me when I did. He told me I could tell them how he felt about their marital situation. Respecting the confidentiality of children's situations can lead to trust in the church in adulthood, making a lifelong difference in their lives. In some cases, where the child's safety is jeopardized, it is vital to let the child know that you have to "tell," because what is happening is wrong. I believe that if a child asks to talk to you, and you suspect a safety issue, it is important to tell the child that you will listen and try to help, but that the help might involve telling other people who can help more.

Obviously, most instances of pastoral care with children happen in or around the context of the family. Martin, for example, shared a family-based problem that was having an effect on many aspects of his life. Most of the help I could offer Martin was through working with the family. Even difficulties with peer relations might have roots in the family. Inclusion of the family in working with children's issues can be done through home visits and informal conversations with the family in other settings, such as fellowship meals or classes. Specific issue-oriented classes for families might also be helpful in your church, with issues determined by the needs of the families of the church. For example, you might organize a class on substance abuse issues for families with children of all ages. Such intergenerational ministry requires a little more attention to learning styles and needs of the various age groups but is very rewarding in terms of participation and response of the families.

Another helpful support for families of the church is a church mentoring or "grandparenting" or similar ministry. In a family mentoring model, families are paired with "grandparents" or other people who have child-rearing experience, and they share experiences and provide guidance. Other family supports include resources such as films, books and tapes, and brochures.

Parenting classes are another type of family support and may take a variety of forms in your church. We offer a weekly class on Sunday morning for parents of young children at my church. They meet to discuss concerns about parenting and family life and have used a variety of resources to assist them. They have also discussed videos on topics ranging from first aid to consumerism. The support and care they receive from the group is probably as important as or more important than the curriculum they study!

There are a good number of resources for use with parenting classes. Your annual conference may have a media library that has videos to be checked out. You can also check with other churches, particularly churches with a Christian educator on staff, to learn about resources with which they have had success.

Methods in classes like these are usually discussion, occasionally lecture, and sometimes storytelling. Another method is to use case studies to examine issues. Like discussing a film or story, reviewing a case study involves looking at a narrative of an event or series of events in relation to a particular issue. Like the story I wrote about Martin, a case study is a short, concise, written report. People reflecting on the case study can share their own wisdom on how they would have or have actually confronted similar issues. It will bring out the experience of the group in professional and educational areas. Finally, since it is a church study or discussion, the group has an opportunity to think about how it is related to Scripture and where God's work is evident in the story. In a parenting class, for example, a family can bring a "case study" of one of their issues. As the group works through it, they provide practical and theological guidance. The entire group has an opportunity for deepening their faith.

Often, you identify difficulties with which you cannot be of much help. Your own skills are limited in the area of pastoral care, and you need to be able to identify these times and refer the family or child to another, more appropriate source of care. When Martin came to me, thinking I could stop the divorce, I told him that I could help his parents find someone who would be good to talk to about it. I am not a marriage counselor, although I have helped many people with marital or premarital problems. I recognize that there are many people more qualified than I am, and I refer people to them. Another side to this issue is a concern about time. Caring for the children is your calling, but only a part of it, and you have to set limits. The limits depend on your own qualifications and calling. My personal general rule is that if I have seen someone three times to discuss their issues, and they still need more help, I refer them to someone who can do longer-term counseling. Referring is still, after all, a type of care you are providing.

When was the last time your church addressed issues of inclusion? Discuss or make a list of the difficult topics your church needs to work on, and brainstorm methods for doing so.

I remember an incident at the beginning of my ministry when a pastor asked me to help out an adolescent by giving her shelter in my home for a night and talking with her. The young woman had some serious problems that I was ill-equipped to deal with, and I was concerned at times for the safety of my family. It was not a well-considered choice on the part of that pastor to refer the adolescent to me, and I didn't have enough knowledge or experience to refuse. I was not the right one to refer this child to. Finding the right person(s) to refer to is a matter of building a file over time. You can begin by asking questions of other staff people or clergy in the area or professional laypeople in your church. Sometimes the referral is to a group rather than a person. For example, over the years I have referred people to Al-Anon (for families of alcoholics) and similar twelve-step groups, CHADD (for families of children with attention deficit disorder), and PFLAG (parents and friends of lesbians and gays). Again, it is important to honor boundaries of confidentiality by getting permission to share relevant facts if you are calling someone else on the child or family's behalf.

At the heart of the support of the church family are issues of inclusion and exclusion. Loving and caring for each one within the diversity of God's kindom is our hope for the church. This means churchwide programs and hard work on racism, sexism, and all of the other "isms" that divide and exclude, as well as welcoming each person as a child of God.

The care of children of the church is a large issue and is a part of all that we do in children's ministries. Most of this chapter has dealt with the response by a single person, pastor, Christian educator, or another person with overall responsibility for the children of the church, but the reality is that care for the children is the responsibility of all people in the church. In all of our classrooms and programs, those of us with organizational responsibility must equip our teachers, other leaders, and members of the community to listen, to advocate, and to share their faith and experiences with the children. The support of a church family not only helps children with specific problems but develops in them an understanding of the church as a family who loves and cares for them. Such an understanding will carry and support our children, even into adulthood, and bring them out of the basement.

Chapter 13
The Beginning

Once Jesus was asked by the Pharisees when the kingdom of God was coming, and he answered, "The kingdom of God is not coming with things that can be observed; nor will they say, 'Look, here it is!' or 'There it is!' For, in fact, the kingdom of God is among you."

Luke 17:20-21

Bringing children's ministries out of the metaphorical basement is not necessarily an easy thing to do, and it's not going to be accomplished in a month or a year or perhaps even a decade. It requires a steady and planned effort, which I hope has been initiated or reinvigorated by your reading of this book. We have covered much ground in the past twelve chapters, trying to describe a holistic approach to ministry with, by, for, and to children within a framework suggested by "A Church for All God's Children." This framework helps us by providing a comprehensive vision for our ministries, and each emphasis (or subsystem) suggests a wide variety of possible ministries within it. To review, the nine emphases identified are:

- Educating the congregation about the needs of children.
- Making church facilities safe and welcoming.
- Reducing the risk of child abuse.
- Helping children grow as faithful disciples.
- Involving children in the life of the church.
- Reaching out to children in the community.

- Advocating legislation and public policies that improve the lives of children and families.
- Relating to children around the world.
- Building administrative supports for ministry with children.

In addition to these nine elements, a holistic system for children's ministry also includes providing pastoral care for children.

All these emphases are important aspects of a holistic children's ministry. And all of them work toward our mission of making disciples of Jesus Christ who will transform the world into the kindom of God. We see glimpses of that kindom among us, even as we journey toward it. It is based on relationships with one another in which the adults of our churches bless, endow, and consecrate our children by living faithfully with them. Those of us who grew up in the church know the great value of these relationships that have formed the faith that we live in our adulthood. I will always thank God for the people of the church in Windom, Minnesota, who blessed, endowed, and consecrated me as a child in their family.

A holistic children's ministry is like a web. All parts are linked together by prayer and concern for the children of the church and world. We do all of this for the sake of the children, that they might grow in faith. All of the areas of the web are interdependent. Changes in one area affect the others in a variety of ways.

Every step we take toward the kindom is important. No step is insignificant. It only takes one person to initiate the first steps toward a holistic ministry with, by, for, and to children. It doesn't matter if you are in a large or small church, in the city or country, a new church or one that has been around for two hundred years. We all have the same mandate to care for the least of these. The way we approach some of the areas of children's ministry will vary according to geographical location, church size, and other demographic variables. But it really doesn't matter how small your church is, or how isolated or how poor. What really matters is gathering the courage and hope to take the first steps out of the basement and onto the first floor of the church's priorities.

My work with children and families in the church leads me to believe we will see many changes in our ministries with children over the next few years. I think we will find new ways to integrate technological advances into our churches. Perhaps we will begin to offer distance-learning options. I am beginning to see a renewed request for intergenerational learning and other ministries, and I believe much of the separation of age groups we currently see in the church will disappear over the next twenty years. New understandings of ministry across the generations will be a cutting edge of church leadership. I also believe that the church will be less and less divided by ministry categories over the next few years. For example, now the efforts of mission work are often separate from education, and evangelism has its own little niche separate from both mission and education. I believe that an integrated approach, where education, mission, and evangelism are components of a particular project, will be a part of the church's future.

The Council of Bishops of The United Methodist Church has asked congregations to evaluate everything they do in terms of its effects on children and the poor. Jesus said to welcome the children, feed his sheep, and care for the least of these. Our mission is to form disciples who will transform the world into the kindom of God. This mission is our mandate for children's ministries.

Outline your church's ministries with, by, for, and to children within the framework suggested by the ten areas listed in this book. Are there specific areas where the church needs to concentrate more efforts? Is one area much more evident than the others? What can you learn from this?

This book does not attempt to cover all of the aspects of children's ministry. There are many good resources that can help you develop specific parts of your children's ministry. There are also many excellent conferences, seminars, and events that provide continuing learning for church leaders. Appendix B lists some good places to start. Learning and support are available in many ways. None of us is alone in our efforts toward a holistic ministry with, by, for, and to children.

This book provides a framework. You can fill in the details. May God bless you and the children in all that you do.

Appendix A
Training Model

One purpose of teacher training is to empower the teachers and leaders so that they might be as good as they possibly can be at their chosen jobs. Satisfaction with their leadership results, in part, from feeling competent. This appendix gives one suggested model for providing training.

Getting Ready

Meet with teachers or leaders at least a week before each unit of study begins. The length of each unit is dependent upon the curriculum resources you use. Many resources are designed in quarterly (approximately thirteen-week) divisions; other resources are in shorter or longer segments.

Select a time that works best for the teachers in your congregation. Some churches use an hour on Sunday morning before classes begin or recruit substitutes and meet during the regularly scheduled class time. In some churches the teachers meet on weeknights.

Invite teachers and leaders each time you meet so that they will feel included, wanted, and reminded. Set up a hospitable environment with refreshments. Provide childcare if needed.

Sample Agenda

The content of the meetings includes information regarding the unit of study, specific skill development, and issues of pastoral care. A general schedule might be:

- Gathering and introductions
- Opening prayer or worship
- Understanding the biblical and theological concepts of the unit of study or program
- Teaching helps
- Specific needs for teaching or leading and extra resources
- Calendar issues
- Concerns for our children
- Sending forth

This format allows for a combination of techniques for providing information and increasing skills. Issues can be discussed, videos may be used to provide "expert" advice, teachers may read some material and then report what they have learned to the entire group, situations may be role-played, and so forth. Modeling a variety of learning methods during these sessions honors the reality that teachers as well as children learn in different ways.

At the first meeting of the year, it is important to focus on procedures and policies that teachers must be aware of. Discuss policies and procedures orally and provide them in written form. These include issues such as:

- First aid and safety procedures
- Evacuation procedures
- Discipline policy
- Child-abuse prevention policy
- Procedures for obtaining new supplies or equipment
- Process for getting a substitute teacher/leader
- Rules about snacks and food
- Recycling and environmental concerns

As the year progresses, you will be able to focus more on discussing pastoral concerns and seasonal/calendar-related items and less on policies and procedures. Other areas that can be explored include methods for teaching and learning, communicating with families, faith development, increased knowledge of the Bible and theology, skills such as story-telling, and so forth.

Beyond the Scheduled Meetings

Regular teachers' meetings don't provide time to develop all of the skills and abilities children's teachers and leaders will need. "On-the-job" training can be provided by pairing experienced teachers with less experienced teachers. New teachers can also be linked with former teachers who will act as supports and mentors. One-on-one training can help new teachers with issues specific to each one's class. E-mail is providing another easy way of being in touch with teachers and can be used to point teachers to any additional resources that have just arrived, remind them of upcoming events and emphases, encourage them throughout the week, and so forth.

There are also opportunities for teacher development beyond the local church. Churches can encourage teachers to take advantage of district, conference, and national seminars and events by providing financial support for registrations and travel. The learning that occurs in these settings often provides a renewed sense of excitement and possibility for children's ministry.

Resources

There are many excellent resources available to help churches develop a holistic approach to children's ministry. The following resources provide a sampling of what is available. While they are listed according to the chapter of this book that they most closely relate to, many of the resources relate to more than one chapter. Resources that are published by Discipleship Resources may be ordered by calling 1-800-685-4370 or visiting the online book store at www.discipleshipresources.org.

Introduction
General Board of Discipleship, P.O. Box 340003, Nashville, TN 37203-0003, 1-877-899-2780. Through resources, events, networks, and research, this general agency of The United Methodist Church supports annual conferences and local churches in the task of making disciples. See the GBOD website (www.gbod.org) for additional information.

The Bishop's Initiative on Children and Poverty. Through this initiative the Bishops of The United Methodist Church call upon United Methodist congregations to undertake actions that will respond to the needs of children and those in poverty. The resource "A Church for All God's Children" supports the initiative. It includes program suggestions and additional resources that relate to the areas of children's ministry discussed in this book. The resource as well as updated information on the initiative can be found at www.umc.org/initiative/.

The Spiritual Life of Children, by Robert Coles (Houghton Mifflin Co., 1990). Images of God and religious persons and events are described by children to a child psychiatrist. Included are prayer, evil, and God's characteristics. This is helpful for understanding children as spiritual beings.

Chapter 1: A Glimpse of the Kin(g)dom

Regarding Children: A New Respect for Childhood and Families, by Herbert Anderson and Susan B. W. Johnson (Westminster John Knox Press, 1994). This is a wonderful resource for understanding the theology behind children's ministries and the value of each child. It would be a great book for a parenting class or for a children's ministry planning group.

Chapter 2: The Body of Christ

Generation to Generation: Family Process in Church and Synagogue, by Edwin H. Friedman (The Guilford Press, 1985). Concepts of family systems are applied to congregations, leadership styles, and congregational dynamics. This is not an easy read, but it is very helpful if you are interested in systems theory.

How Your Church Family Works: Understanding Congregations as Emotional Systems, by Peter L. Steinke (The Alban Institute, 1993). This book gives the basics of emotional systems in congregations, helpful in understanding relationships in the church.

When a Butterfly Sneezes: A Guide for Helping Kids Explore Interconnections in Our World Through Favorite Stories, by Linda Booth Sweeny (Pegasus Communications, 2001). A guide to introduce children to systems thinking.

Chapter 3: Teaching the Whole Church

Foundations: Shaping the Ministry of Christian Education in Your Congregation (Discipleship Resources, 1993). It describes the biblical and theological foundations of teaching and learning in The United Methodist Church.

Putting Children and Their Families First: A Planning Handbook For Congregations, by Laura Dean Ford Friedrich (General Board of Global Ministries, 1997). This planning handbook for assessing the needs of children helps a congregation plan and meet the needs of the community through ministry. It has lots of information and ideas, with worship and prayer suggestions.

Chapter 4: The First Three Things

The Child Friendly Church: 150 Models of Ministry With Children, by Boyce A. Bowden (Abingdon Press, 1999). Practical models are provided by churches who are in ministry with children in a variety of ways. It includes personal and church names of real people and programs that can be resources for you.

The First Three Years: A Guide for Infants, Toddlers, and Two-Year-Olds, edited by Mary Alice Gran (Discipleship Resources, 2001). This book follows a basic, nuts-and-bolts approach to ministry with our youngest members, including articles on safety, organization, supplies, and more.

God, Kids and Us: The Growing Edge of Ministry With Children and the People Who Care for Them, by Janet Marshall Eibner and Susan Graham Walker (Morehouse Publishing, 1997). A great "how-to" resource, it has lots of examples of forms and illustrations and chapters on recruitment and evaluation.

Welcome the Child: A Child Advocacy Guide for Churches, by Shannon Daley and Kathleen Guy (Friendship Press and Children's Defense Fund, 1994). This is a basic guide for anyone involved in children's ministries, detailing the mandate for child advocacy in our churches. It is a good source of worship materials for inclusion of children and concerns about children in worship. (Available from the Children's Defense Fund.)

Chapter 5: Not in My Church

A Child Called It: An Abused Child's Journey from Victim to Victor, by Dave Pelzer (Health Communications, Inc., 1995). An account of the life's story of Dave Pelzer, a survivor of severe child abuse by his mother, it is hard (very sad) to read but helpful in understanding the depth of the problem and the importance of adults in his life.

Bless Our Children: Preventing Sexual Abuse, Center for the Prevention of Sexual and Domestic Violence, 936 N. 34th Street, #200, Seattle, WA 98103. 206-634-1903. This is a video relating to curriculum resources for use with children in preventing child abuse. It includes a detailed description of a program in a local church.

Center for the Prevention of Sexual and Domestic Violence, 936 N. 34th Street, #200, Seattle, WA 98103. 206-634-1903. www.cpsdv.org. The center produces videos and other resources. In addition to the child-abuse work they have done, there are great resources on domestic violence and the religious response to it.

Hear Their Cries: Religious Responses to Child Abuse, Center for the Prevention of Sexual and Domestic Violence, 936 N. 34th Street, #200, Seattle, WA 98103. 206-634-1903. This video, a general overview of abuse in the church and congregation, is aimed at clergy, with helpful information on procedures and case studies.

National Safety Council website (www.nsc.org). This website provides a wide variety of information related to health and safety.

Prevent Child Abuse America, 200 S. Michigan Ave., 17th Floor, Chicago, IL 60604-2404. 312-663-3520. www.preventchildabuse.org. This is a source of facts about child abuse, parenting tips, and resources.

Reducing the Risk, a resource kit from *Church Law and Tax Report,* Christian Ministry Resources, P.O. Box 2301, Matthews, NC 28106. 800-222-1840. This kit contains a video, an audio tape, a reference book, and a training manual for local churches to use in education policy making in the church on child sexual abuse. It details procedures for risk reduction, including screening, policies, and prevention.

Safe Sanctuaries: Reducing the Risk of Child Abuse in the Church, by Joy Thornburg Melton (Discipleship Resources, 1998). This is a "must have" for anyone in ministry with children in The United Methodist Church. This book helps churches develop policies and procedures to reduce risk. Sample forms and policies for use in the local church are included.

National Center on Child Abuse and Neglect website (www.ojjdp.ncjrs.org/pubs/fedresources/ag-05.html). This agency is a part of the U.S. Department of Health and Human Services.

Community resources relating to the prevention of child abuse include your police department, your church's insurance company, and other churches in your community.

Chapter 6: Growing as Disciples

The Children's God, by David Heller (University of Chicago Press, 1986). This book is wonderfully descriptive of ways in which children understand God at various ages. It presents some differences in children's concepts of God based on gender and religious background as well as on age.

Gender Gaps: Where Schools Still Fail Our Children, by The American Association of University Women (Marlowe and Co., 1999). This is an update of the study called "How Schools Shortchange Girls" that drew nationwide attention to the idea of a gender gap in education. Filled with information and data, it is not easy to read but has relevance if you have interest in the topic.

Forecast is the quarterly catalog by Cokesbury that includes approved United Methodist curriculum. A wide variety of curriculum resources are offered that are based on the philosophy described in *Foundations: Shaping the Ministry of Christian Education in Your Congregation* (listed above with the resources for Chapter 3).

How Do Our Children Grow? Introducing Children to God, Jesus, the Bible, Prayer, and Church, by Delia Halverson (Chalice Press, 1999). This is a practical guide to helping children understand faith concepts, with a study guide for parents, teachers, and other leaders.

Seven Ways of Teaching the Bible to Children, by Barbara Bruce (Abingdon Press, 1996). This book is a clear and usable description of children's learning styles applied to Christian education.

Sprouts: Nurturing Children Through Covenant Discipleship, by Edie Genung Harris and Shirley Ramsey (Discipleship Resources, 1996). This book helps congregations develop Covenant Discipleship Groups appropriate for children.

Teaching Young Children: A Guide for Teachers and Leaders, revised edition, by MaryJane Pierce Norton (Discipleship Resources, 1997). This little book is full of good ideas for teaching and leading infants and young children. It includes many practical how-to ideas on topics such as equipment needs and appropriate toys.

Teaching Godly Play: The Sunday Morning Handbook, by Jerome Berryman (Abingdon Press, 1995). It describes an approach where children experience the story and then independently choose a means of expressing it or incorporating it into their lives.

Workshop Rotation: A New Model for Sunday School, by Melissa Armstrong-Hansche and Neil MacQueen (Geneva Press, 2000). This is an easy-to-read basic manual on the workshop rotation method for Sunday class organization. It gives lots of ideas for further exploration of rotation and a rationale for changing to this story-based model.

Chapter 7: And a Child Shall Lead
Capture the Moment: Building Faith Traditions for Families, by Rick and Sue Isbell (Discipleship Resources, 1998). The book identifies a wide variety of life events and provides suggestions on how families can make faith connections with the events.

Children Worship! by MaryJane Pierce Norton (Discipleship Resources, 1997). This is a worship education resource for congregational use.

Hand in Hand: Growing Spiritually With Our Children, by Sue Downing (Discipleship Resources, 1998). Offers help for parents as they raise their children as Christian disciples.

Touch the Water, Taste the Bread (Cokesbury, 1998). A set of resources to teach preschoolers and elementary-aged children and their parents about the sacraments, it includes teachers' guides and supplemental resources for crafts, drama, and more.

Chapter 8: Children on the Playground
Ecumenical Child Care Network. This is a national organization that promotes quality early childhood care and advocates education for all children. Write for membership information at ECCN, 8765 West Higgins Road, Suite 450, Chicago, IL 60631 or visit their website at www.eccn.org.

FaithHome for Parents, edited by Sally Sharpe (Abingdon Press, 1999). This is a series of brochures on parenting and family issues, with topics ranging from new parents' information to blended families. Up-to-date lists of resources are included in each.

It Takes a Village: And Other Lessons Children Teach Us, by Hillary Rodham Clinton (Simon and Schuster, 1996). With thoughtful advocacy for the role of society in children's lives and in meeting the needs of children today, this is a good book for discussions of issues.

Kids Count website (www.aecf.org/kidscount/). This website is sponsored by the Annie E. Casey Foundation. It includes the *Kids Count Data Book* and Online Database. These resources provide excellent demographic information about children and youth.

National Association for the Education of Young Children (NAEYC). 1509 16th Street NW, Washington, DC 20036. Website: www.naeyc.org. This organization is committed to improving early childhood education.

Chapter 9: A Voice for the Voiceless
The United Methodist Child Advocacy Network provides resources and ideas to help members be more effective advocates for children. You can enroll as a member of this network online at www.umc-gbcs.org/network1.htm or by mail at General Board of Church and Society, 100 Maryland Avenue NE, Washington, DC 20002.

Children's Defense Fund, P.O. Box 90500 Washington, DC 20090-0500. 202-628-8787. www.childrensdefense.org. This is a child advocacy organization that promotes legislative change and publishes many resources related to children and child advocacy, including the Children's Sabbath worship resources. A good source of current statistical information can be found in their annual publication called *The State of America's Children Yearbook*.

National Center for Children in Poverty website (http://cpmcnet. columbia.edu/dept/nccp/index.html). This website includes statistics on children in poverty.

Connect for Kids: Guidance for Grown-ups (www.connectforkids.org). This is a website sponsored by the Benton Foundation. It provides a resource for adults who want to build better communities for children and families. It includes up-to-date information on national issues affecting the well-being of children.

Chapter 10: These Are Our Children, Too

ABCs: *Advance Book of Children's Projects*, General Board of Global Ministries. The Advance Office, 475 Riverside Drive, Room 1400, New York, NY 10115. This is a free booklet listing and describing projects around the world related to children's well-being. Additional information and resources from the General Board of Global Ministries can be found at http://gbgm-umc.org/.

Child to Child Program, International Child Care USA, 3620 North High Street, Suite 110, Columbus, OH 43214. 1-800-722-4453. Website: www.gospelcom.net/iccl. Teacher's guide and six lesson/activity resources are available for use with children to help them understand mission and respond with support for the children of Haiti. The resource headings are Compassion, Health and Hope, Involvement, Love, and Discipleship.

Church World Service, 28606 Phillips Street, P.O. Box 968, Elkhart, IN 46515. www.churchworldservice.org/. This ministry of the National Council of Churches publishes a variety of resources on children around the world, especially related to hunger and nutrition.

"The Children's Fund for Christian Mission" packet, published annually. This free packet gives useful project descriptions and teaching/learning activities for children of all ages and includes a map. The packet may be requested from United Methodist Children's Fund for Christian Mission, P.O. Box 340013, Nashville, TN 37203-0013. Additional information about the Children's Fund can be found at http://gbgm-umc.org/kc/.

United States Committee for UNICEF (United Nations Children's Fund), 333 East 38th Street, New York, NY 10016. Go to www.unicefusa.org for the U.S. committee's website or www.unicef.org for the international organization's website. The committee offers various publications and resources to assist with understanding the life situations of children of the world.

Chapter 11: Making It Stick

Children's Ministries: Ministries That Help Children Grow in Faith, by Mary Alice Gran (Cokesbury, 2000). This booklet is part of the *Guidelines for Leading Your Congregation* series. It provides help in planning and organizing children's ministry.

Children's Teacher, published by Cokesbury. This quarterly resource provides helps for Sunday School teachers and other children's leaders on a wide variety of topics.

Keeping In Touch: Christian Formation and Teaching, by Carol F. Krau (Discipleship Resources, 1999). This book describes five critical processes for teachers and leaders.

Now Is the Time! by Craig Kennet Miller (Discipleship Resources, 1999). This video, which comes with a discussion guide, describes key characteristics of the Millennial Generation.

Chapter 12: Caring for the Children

Children and Adults with Attention-Deficit/Hyperactivity Disorder (CHADD), 8181 Professional Place, Suite 201, Landover, MD 20785. 800-233-4050. www.chadd.org. This is a national support and educational organization.

Helping Children Cope With Divorce, by Jenni Douglas Duncan (Discipleship Resources, 1999). This is a congregational approach to supporting children whose parents are divorcing or who have experienced divorces. Includes reproducible activities and games, leader's guide, and parents' sessions.

Helping Children Grieve: When Someone They Love Dies, by Theresa Huntley (Augsburg Fortress Press, 1991). This is a very good resource for helping children deal with death.

Parents, Families and Friends of Lesbians and Gays (PFLAG), 1726 M Street NW, Suite 400, Washington, DC 20036. 202-467-8180. www.pflag.org. This is a support and education group. Many resources are available through local and state chapters of PFLAG.

Pastoral Care With Children in Crisis, by Andrew D. Lester (Westminster Press, 1985). A primary book for persons engaged in pastoral care of children, it gives the mandate to care and includes suggestions for techniques in reaching children.

The Pastoral Care of Children, by Daniel H. Grossoehme (Haworth Pastoral Press, 1999). This is a particularly helpful guide for caring for children by persons who aren't necessarily comfortable with children. It offers good tips on specific difficulties of children and has a wonderful annotated bibliography.

Chapter 13: The Beginning

Guide My Feet: Prayers and Meditations on Loving and Working for Children, by Marian Wright Edelman (Beacon Press, 1995). A wonderful source of inspiration for all of us who love children, this book includes prayers, poems, and stories and an index to first lines.

A Prayer for Children (Children's Defense Fund, 1996). Three minutes long. This video, available from the Children's Defense Fund, contains Ina Hughes' poem about the needs of children, read by Marian Wright Edelman, with footage of children.